Why Dolphins Jump

A Picture Book of the
Acrobats of the Sea

Ann Weaver, Ph.D.

JAASAS ACADEMIC PRESS

JA

DIVERSIFIED EXPLORATION AND
EDUCATION SERVICES

Weaver, Ann. (2020). Why Dolphins Jump – A picture book of the acrobats of the sea. Jaasas Academic Press. Treasure Island, FL. ISBN-13 978-0-578-65242-9.

Dedicated to the dolphin we call Diana:
The seas still shine, but you took their sparkle when you left.

Table of Contents

Foreword

Ann Weaver is fascinated with why dolphins jump because the subject lies along the misty edges of advancing knowledge while her adept storytelling maintains the rapt attention of her readers (Picture 1).

In my view, the encyclopedic scope of her delightful picture book moves the topic well beyond those amorphous edges by weaving together countless fragments into a coherent fabric for both professional and public consumption. I was easily absorbed in my first read, and experience continuing intrigue as her beguiling explanations of dolphin behavior bring new insights into my own work.

I am an animal behaviorist and anthrozoologist, studying the science behind animal learning and human-animal interactions and relationships. I have specialized in teaching both terrestrial and marine animals, and their human caregivers, for more than two decades. I co-founded an animal welfare and behavior consulting firm, Precision Behavior, in 2009 which continues to advise zoos and aquariums globally. Correspondingly, I write this Foreword in my view 'from the pool.' Along the continuum of understanding dolphin behavior, I stand on one end among human-managed dolphins and Ann Weaver stands on the other end in her boat at sea among free-ranging dolphins. Yet, as if hailing each other from a distance, as the dolphins themselves do at sea, *Why Dolphins Jump* strikes a number of resonant chords that illustrate the positive potential of cross-fertilization between the professions of zoological animal training and field ethology.

For example, the startling story about the plotting pilot whale (Picture 2) takes place in an oceanarium. In setting the stage, the text states candidly that, at the time, zoo animals had unvarying daily routines. Today, that is no longer entirely true. Although some zoo animals today have lives that are far more routine than I would personally like, many zoos – certainly the zoos that my company consults with – work hard to make each day variable for the animals because we recognize the animals' needs for mental stimulation. Modern husbandry strategies and progressive zoo leaders work to promote animal psychological well-being in a way never before seen in a history that began with animal menageries for the edification of the wealthy. *Why Dolphins Jump* can become a treasured resource in the interests of promoting public education and animal mental health.

At one point in the text, I stumbled over a reference to a dolphin as an "it" instead of as a "him" or a "her" (Picture 151). This particular reference caused me pause, because zoo animals are rarely an "it." It's far easier for us to assess who is male and who is female. Yet, at sea, a free-ranging dolphin may remain an "it" for years, or forever, because of the difficulties of identifying gender from boat-based observations. The idea that it is still admissible to call a free-ranging dolphin "it," nay, frequently unavoidable, is likely to be an alien concept to many people who work with animals in zoos or aquariums. Knowing gender is a gift, not a guarantee, at least on the seaside end of the continuum. I had never considered that gender identification of a free-ranging dolphin at sea is among the most demanding of field accomplishments, let alone systematically generating the age-sex profile of an entire dolphin community. I never realized how this "simple information" requires an unfathomable investment of time, necessarily girded by researcher presence and attention at the precise moment when the dolphin performs the revealing aerial behavior. Then there is the added necessity of having one's camera poised to document that fleeting moment. Moreover, today's preference for referring to an animal as he or she instead of "it" is a *very* recent phenomenon, as are its ramifications for respecting an animal as the individual ambassador from a foreign society that he or she is. Last but not least, *Why Dolphins Jump* is based on 15 years of research. Science demands evidence. In this case, that demands a perfectly focused photo of the lower abdomen of a wild dolphin while he or she dances atop distant waves! Few types of pictures are harder to obtain (Picture 33), highlighting the value of both in-situ and ex-situ study. We simply cannot learn everything in zoo-based research nor in wild setting observations.

I found it interesting that free-ranging dolphins may jump to regain researchers' attention (Picture 18). A reasonable hypothesis from such observations is that free-ranging dolphins receive some reinforcing value from the researchers' return. That's how behavior is tested and how positive reinforcement works. The fascinating point here is that trainers do everything within their power to build relationships with the animals for whom they care, to make themselves as interesting and valuable as possible. We want the dolphins (or any other animal in our care) to recognize us and to want to interact with us – it's all about bonded relationships. In contrast, the *opposite is true* of ethological field work. Most studies of free-ranging animal behavior require researchers to remain as neutral and unobtrusive as possible to minimize animal behavior change due to researcher presence. So too is the goal of Ann's study: understand as much as possible about dolphin behavior on their terms. Whereas no one can be secretive in a boat trailing dolphins, Ann feels that researcher presence is reinforcing in some situations but not in others; thus, an important part of her job is to recognize this difference and behave accordingly to collect sound scientific data yet treat the dolphins fairly in the process. The latter point is more than mere sentiment. Her non-negotiable field edict is to establish trust to have good access; harassed dolphins are hard to approach again and impossible to observe at length. Yet the fact that the dolphins actively seek to gain her attention must indicate some level of trust, again bridging the gap between dolphins who live in these different contexts. Ann operates with a full understanding, however, that scientific data collection protocols must be followed as consistently as humanly possible; inconsistent data collection renders a study impotent. She also notes that most observational bouts seem to have a natural stopping point, that she sees as a reflection of the "Ok, see you later" psychology of fission fusion social structures.

Another intriguing counterpoint relates to observations of aerial breaching and general writhing among heavily pregnant dolphins at sea (Picture 70). Pregnant dolphins in aquariums frequently slide out on their bellies, maybe for the same reason. This is yet another good example of how captive work informs field work, and vice versa.

There are more fascinating counterpoints, but I will stop with a final example of high spy-hopping behavior (Picture 136). The dolphin in the picture, Sylvia, appears to be tail-walking, a commonly taught behavior in marine parks and one that spread among free-ranging Australian dolphins after a trained dolphin was released back into the sea. But Sylvia is not tail-walking. Ann has never seen tail-walking among free-ranging dolphins, providing a potential example of a behavior that is not performed without training but which if animals are taught to do by humans or other dolphins, and if they find fun or reinforcing in some way, they may choose to do of their own accord (as the Australian dolphins demonstrated). This is unsurprising, certainly to Ann, who has invested so much of her life studying these social cognitive animals in their own 'enchanted river' in Florida.

Cross-fertilization between human-managed animal training and field ethology is too rare, and I finished this book wanting more. *Why Dolphins Jump* is a short, stout foot bridge between the two fields. I hope, and suspect, it will be well-traveled.

Angi Millwood Lacinak, M.A.
Founder, Precision Behavior

Preface: Welcome Aboard the "Enchanted River"

PICTURE 1

*Bottlenose dolphins are among the greatest social intellects on Earth.
The subject of why they jump lies along the misty edge of advancing knowledge, all the more tantalizing for its fragmentary nature.*

What release to write so that one forgets oneself, forgets one's companion, forgets where one is or what one is going to do next – to be drenched in work as one is drenched in sleep or in the sea.

Anne Morrow Lindbergh: Gift of the Sea

For the lucky people on boats at sea, it is thrilling to see dolphins – even more thrilling to see dolphins jump. Jumping dolphins are often playing. More often, jumps have meaning far beyond play. Dolphin jumps are broadcasts of note among intelligent individuals who survive by sending and receiving important broadcasts at crucial moments. A person who knows why a dolphin jumps has an elusive alphabet all the more alluring for its obscurity – a Rosetta Stone of dolphin communication.

Why Dolphins Jump was inspired by the many sailing clubs of St. Petersburg, Florida, that invited me to explain the behavior of bottlenose dolphins, *Tursiops truncatus,* that they might see from their boats. I am an ethologist, an animal behaviorist fascinated by how nature has carved animals to live. In addition to working with over 200 animal species so far, mostly mammals[1], I am also fortunate to have studied bottlenose dolphins in five different seas (off San Diego in Southern California, Outer Banks off North Carolina, Gulf of California off Baja California Sur, northwest banks off Grand Bahama, and St. Petersburg in west central Florida). Because jumping is the most memorable dolphin behavior, I started adding pictures of jumping dolphins to my talks from my 120,000 photo archive. The growing list of pictures and explanations, and this book, shows that dolphins jump for a stunning number of different reasons, only one of which is play.

This book is mostly drawn from my 15-year Florida study to identify how coastal construction impacts coastal dolphins. From 2004 through this writing in 2019, I have gone out in a small boat 2-4 times a week and made a detailed record of the dolphins' behavior before, during, and after a 5-year construction project to replace an old bridge over vital dolphin habitat called John's Pass (National Oceanic and Atmospheric Administration, NOAA, research permits 1088-1815, 16299, and 20346).

I wrote *Why Dolphins Jump* for a general audience and made all of its observations, took all of its photos, and generated its interpretations. I have not cited authorities because citations are suited to technical reports and break the flow of the text. Yet I would err greatly if I failed to acknowledge the inspiring influence of many brilliant biologists and ethologists I have known personally or through their works who shaped my thinking and therefore my interpretations of why dolphins jump.

I also thank specific people for particularly memorable discussions of animal behavior. In alphabetical order: Alan Alda, Alexis Cancemi, Beth Brady, Bill Clough, Briana Seay Harvey, Cara Gubbins, Carolyn Cush, Dian Fossey, Emma Spada, Filipo Aureli, Frans de Waal, Hans Kummer, Karen and Martisha, Ken Norris, Kirsten Smail, Jan van Hooff, Jane Goodall, Josep Call, Lesley Ferguson, Marc Bekoff, Maureen and Brandon Duryee, Mike Seres, Peter Verbeek, Randy Wells, Richard Connor, Saskia Arendt, Shauna McBride-Kebert, Stan Kuczaj, and Susie Ekard. I thank countless more supporters who helped when needed, including NOAA and FWC scientists, the Lindvall family, and my esteemed Good-natured Statistics Consulting clients, whose win-win-win collaborations also help support this research.

I primarily acknowledge Captain John Heidemann: His tireless support, devoted driving around the dolphins, and diligent boat maintenance made this study possible. I deeply appreciate the loyal support of the rest of my family: Larry, Marge, Mary, John, and Paul Weaver. Special thanks to Kirsten Smail, Amy Walters, Marie Dahlberg, and Casey Hamel for help with data collection. Deep thanks to my thoughtful book reviewers: Angi Millwood Lacinak, Kirsten Smail, Amy Sophie White, Sandy Morrissette, and Doris Eaton. Sincere thanks to my editor, Don Kerr, for his patient and powerful wordsmithing. Photo credits were removed intentionally for artistic effect, but the photos are numbered and available for purchase from DolphinsDigital.org.

Our 14,000 encounters with free-ranging Florida dolphins have revealed many reasons why dolphins jump. I hope you find their reasons as fascinating as I do. Welcome aboard!

Ann Weaver, Ph.D.

Good-natured Statistics Consulting

Discreet and Friendly Data Handling Services – Even Friendlier Prices!
(GoodNaturedStatistics.com)

Other books by this author:

Secrets behind the Dolphin Smile – 25 Amazing Things Dolphins Do

Clinical Biostatistics and Epidemiology Made Ridiculously Simple
(with Steve Goldberg, M.D.)

Good-Natured Statistics in Everyday Language with Animal Behavior

CHAPTER 1

Personal Introduction to Why Dolphins Jump

A jumping dolphin always has its reasons for jumping. It was not, however, a dolphin who taught me this. It was a pilot whale, as long and gleaming as a shiny black limousine but far more calculating.

I was part of a team studying captive dolphins at Sea World San Diego. To do this, we stood at the edge of a large pool swirling with animated, gray, 8-foot bottlenose dolphins and their large, jet-black cousins, 19-foot pilot whales with big round heads and small bright eyes.

Like most zoo animals at the time, the dolphins and pilot whales had a mostly unchanging daily routine in their pool. Stationed silently at poolside in those hushed hours before the park opened, we were a change in their routine and therefore a curiosity to them. Likewise, they to me. Soft at dawn, the sea air was fragrant from the blossoms that carpeted the park. It was quiet except for the sloshing water in the pool where the mysterious air-breathing

PICTURE 2

This captive pilot whale has learned to jump for a fish reward. Pilot whales are between bottlenose dolphins and orca (killer whales) in size. Individuals can be recognized by the unique shape of the light-colored saddle behind the dorsal fin.

1

PICTURE 3
*Instead of diving back in neatly, a **breaching** dolphin lands on the water surface flatly. Flat landings create big splashes and plenty of noise, which is quite handy at times.*

sea creatures swam ceaselessly, their blowholes blinking like eyes and filling the air with sighing breaths.

This exotic, sensory-rich environment required concentration to collect the systematic information that qualifies as data. So we were taught to focus on one dolphin at a time, a technique called a focal animal sample. The idea was to ignore the other dolphins and whales in the pool unless they interacted with one's focal dolphin.

Accordingly, I ignored the massive black pilot whale who cruised back and forth in front of me, even when it kept lifting its big round head above the water surface to peer at me with small bright eyes. I was an easy target standing at the edge of that pool, especially because I did not yet know that dolphins and their big cousins might think in terms of targets.

After many minutes of being ignored, the gleaming black whale shot into the air like a torpedo and dropped flatly onto the water in a massive body slam right in front of me. This created a huge splash that covered me with icy pool water!

As I sprang back, I realized that the "water" that hit my stomach was warm.

The whale I ignored had urinated on me!

It seems to me that the whale understood rejection and revenge.

Now years later, no longer poolside, I stand in a small boat and study free-ranging bottlenose dolphins in Florida seas. None has sent a sheet of warm "water" over me like that calculating pilot whale. Then again, I have not ignored the dolphins, either. In 14,000 encounters, they have revealed many reasons why they jump.

Have you ever wondered why dolphins jump?

PICTURE 4

The astonishment and pleasure of people watching dolphins jump out of their boat's wake is obvious. Jumping and surfing dolphins are thrilling to see at sea.

CHAPTER 2

Attitudes behind the Aerials

B ottlenose dolphins are the only animals I know who come out of nature to help and to play with people, and we love them for it. Between playing and that famous smile, it is easy to think that dolphins are carefree and always happy. Not true. Dolphins face the same challenges to survival that all animals face in nature. Although dolphins *are* more playful than most animals, they do not play all the time. Along these lines, jumping dolphins are not automatically playing.

PICTURE 5

*A jump is a type of aerial behavior. An **aerial behavior** is any maneuver that shows more of the dolphin's body out of the water than the standard breathing surface. The **double spyhop** in this picture is a pretty behavior where bodies bump as dolphins shove each other sideways. It occurs during play and fighting.*

PICTURE 6

*We watch the exotic world of free-ranging bottlenose dolphins in our **study area**, a 6.5-mile (10.5 km) stretch of west central Florida's Intracoastal Waterway. This aerial view of the study area shows heavy human habitation but tends to hide the long stretches of natural coastline that nonetheless remain, unhardened by sea walls. In my view, these waterways manage to support life from diatoms to dolphins because of the long stretches of natural coastline.*

The Intracoastal Waterway winds between the mainland and barrier islands, swelling into broad bays and squeezing into narrow ribbons of water. During 15 years of searching this stretch over and over for dolphins, it became the "Enchanted River" for me. I like the nickname because it reminds me that its enchanting glimpses of the dolphins' captivating society can be obtained wherever bottlenose dolphins are found.

Free-ranging bottlenose dolphins use aerial behaviors for many reasons besides play: to express affection, irritation, excitement, anger, and especially avoidance. Dolphins use aerial behaviors to show off, tease each other, retaliate, test the mettle of rivals, establish social rank, settle political disputes, give and get a better look, and fight. This book offers a glimpse of that exotic world.

Aerial Behavior across the Dolphin Lifespan

Dolphins use aerial behaviors for different reasons across their life time. Bottlenose dolphins of the "Enchanted River" also jump any time of year. However, jumping varies with the numbers of dolphins, and those numbers vary across the seasons. We see the fewest dolphins in winter, the most in summer. Because the presence of other dolphins is exciting and excited dolphins tend to jump, dolphins tend to jump more often during the summer than in other seasons. Aerial behaviors are also more frequent in summer because summer seas are warm and energy conservation is unnecessary. Dolphin excitement varies from light-hearted, as in play, to tense, as in conflict.

Bottlenose dolphins are highly social animals. Rarely alone, they have rich communication systems. Jumping is a part of communication, a dolphin Rosetta Stone, if you will. All dolphins can jump, but not all do. Similar to the way people show individual tendencies to dance or not, dolphins show individual tendencies to jump or not. Some dolphins are particularly "jumpy." Yet, others will only jump if goaded into it.

Bottlenose dolphins gather in small to large groups whose members change regularly. This is a form of social organization called a fission fusion society, fission for breaking apart and fusion for coming together. The rich social life that this creates takes brains to manage because a dolphin has to keep track of a large number of relationships. For example, in just the modest stretch of the "Enchanted River" that we monitor, a dolphin associates with over 100 other dolphins. Yet they also travel extensively outside of our study area. Therefore, a dolphin may know hundreds of other dolphins. In doing so, a dolphin must mentally store a tremendous amount of information.

Bottlenose dolphins may live up to 60 years. They jump at all ages. Many of the dolphins leaping across these pages are in their 20s or 30s, impressive ages for free-ranging animals living in nature without modern medicine. Because dolphins can live for several decades, each life stage (calf, adolescent or teenager, and adult) is long too. Dolphins in each stage have their own reasons for jumping.

Females give birth to a calf every four years on average. Pregnancy lasts a year. Heavily pregnant females occasionally jump with great vigor. Of all of the secrets the dolphins

PICTURE 7
*Puck is a particularly jumpy dolphin. Forming a beautiful arc called a **bow** against summer seas, in this picture he leaps to catch his breath during a tussle with other teens.*

have shared about why they jump, the pregnant females' reasons for jumping remain the most mysterious.

Calf survival is high in the "Enchanted River." The first aerial behavior of the newborn dolphin is called a *darting breath*. I use darting breaths to broadly assess the newborn's health and well-being. Babies who dart too often or extremely tend to die young, as if their fresh little engines were revving too much or the noise and splashing from their uncontrolled zeal attracted sharks, whose acute hearing allows them to detect splashing from great distances. Mother dolphins are extremely attentive to their babies and are stricken should the baby die.

PICTURE 8
Diana's two-month-old calf Denver wells up out of calm seas during a
darting breath.

Bottlenose dolphin calves mature exceptionally early in some respects and exceptionally late in other respects. For example, they begin to practice fishing and sexual techniques while they are still nursing mother's milk. Yet they remain with mom for many years after they have ceased nursing, up to seven years altogether. Calves tend to jump many times in a row, although their reasons, revealed throughout this book, are surprising. When sufficiently provoked, mothers jump to discipline their kids… often to make them stop jumping!

After a grown calf leaves its mother (weans) and lives independently, it is called an adolescent, subadult, or teenager. Females spend 3-6 years as teenagers or until they have their first calf, whereupon we call them adults. Males probably spend two to three times that long as teenagers or until they father their first calf, whereupon we call them adults. However, we do not know the ages of bulls at first fatherhood because we have yet to collect the genetic samples needed to identify family ties.

Male and female teenagers of the "Enchanted River" jump for different reasons. Bottlenose bulls build large, complex dominance networks, so teen males devote their time to carving out their spot in this fascinating society within a society. Jumping plays a significant role as bulls debate, establish, and renegotiate their relationships with one another based on their personal strength and spirit, as well as support from allies. Bulls of all ages use a veritable arsenal of jumps across time as strengthening young bulls ascend the social ladder and weakening old bulls descend it. I broadly distinguish younger, lower-ranking *junior bulls* from older, higher-ranking *senior bulls*.

During their teen years, most maturing males also establish a deep relationship with another male. These are formally called *alliance*s and informally called *bonded bull buddies*. These relationships are intense because, once in place, bonded bulls will spend 99% of their time together, often for decades or the rest of their lives. These long-term alliances of bonded bulls are almost unique in the animal kingdom. Somewhat like modern marriages, a teen bull may try on several different bulls for size before establishing a long-term bond. Jumping plays a large role in these tryouts too.

Teen females mainly jump to avoid males. Female dolphins on the "Enchanted River" take several years to mature sexually, during which they must learn about the nature of bull attention because it does not appear to be instinctive. My observations suggest that most teen females have mixed feelings about males. In contrast, males understand sex by the time they wean from their mothers because they have been practicing since they were calves.

Telling Dolphins Apart - Dorsal Fin Differences

Like any good soap opera, observers have to be able to tell the players apart. Similarly, to follow the plots of life at sea, dolphin behaviorists like me have to recognize individual

PICTURE 9

The bottlenose dolphin dorsal fin serves as a sword, shield, and chew toy. Although the fin is made of tough cartilage, these activities damage it over time, as Bruce's scalloped dorsal fin illustrates here. Dolphins with unique notch patterns or other scars can be identified individually. We have identified 418 dolphins to date. They are included in the Gulf of Mexico Dolphin Identification System (GoMDIS; NOAA OBIS Seamap).

dolphins on sight. This is possible because most bottlenose dolphins develop a unique pattern on the fin that sits on its back like a sail, the dorsal fin, making that individual distinct from other dolphins.

Identifying a dolphin as an individual by its dorsal fin is a separate accomplishment from identifying it as a male or female, because a person looking at a dolphin swimming past a boat cannot say with certainty whether it is a male or a female. We have to see the dolphin's genitals to identify its gender. This has taken as long as 8 years on the "Enchanted River" and, in about a half of the cases, is never accomplished. As a result, I use the pronouns 'he' or 'she' only for dolphins whose gender I have identified. Otherwise, I refer to it as 'it' in this book.

Historic descriptions of natural history are rife with elaborate fabrications built from the slender edifice of one or two observations. To avoid this pitfall, I have based each of my interpretations on careful consideration of hundreds of observations of each behavior described herein, and the context(s) in which it occurred. To that end, I have taken great pains to avoid anthropomorphism, the incorrect explanation of an animal's behavior by equating it to human behavior. The parallels that I do draw between dolphins and humans are, to my knowledge, fair.

Although *Why Dolphins Jump* is based on research, I have exercised artistic license to make it easier to read. I replaced each dolphin's scientific code with a human name. For example, in Picture 9, Bruce's real name is JP5BB-DBLU-4710. I also replaced technical terms with their descriptive cousins, such as replacing COA40+ with the word 'friends.' However, dolphins think and act like dolphins. Their rules of conduct are not human rules. They are not people in dolphin suits.

Basic Types of Jumps

Aerial behaviors fall into seven categories of maneuvers that show more of the dolphin's body out of the water than the standard breathing surface: bows, T-bones, breaches, leaps, slaps, spyhops, and surfing. I included surfing boats because surfing dolphins often jump. Although many dolphin social exchanges are complex and combine different types of jumps, each type of aerial behavior has a separate chapter in this book.

Bows, T-bones, breaches, and leaps are basic types of jumps. They differ in how the body is held and what they accomplish. The jumping dolphin can leave the water entirely and show all of its body or leave the water partially and show only part of its body. For example, slapping and spyhopping dolphins usually show only parts of their body.

An aerial behavior may or may not directly involve a second dolphin. However, given that dolphins on the "Enchanted River" are usually in the company of other dolphins and usually jump when in the company of other dolphins, it seems to me that most aerial behaviors are social statements. Moreover, healthy dolphins move constantly. In my view, movement itself has evolved into one of the dolphins' richest forms of communication. Aerial behaviors play a large role in the art of dolphin communication.

It is often difficult to know why a dolphin suddenly jumps out of the water. One reason for this difficulty is the sleek torpedo-shape of the dolphin body. Its streamlining limits the number

PICTURE 10
Streamlining refers to the torpedo shape of the dolphin body.

of different moves that a dolphin is physically capable of performing. Shaped like a torpedo, a dolphin can only physically perform about a hundred moves. Consequently, dolphins use the same aerial behaviors in different social settings. For example, the double spyhop shown on Picture 5 is a mutual, vertical shoving match used playfully but also aggressively. In addition, each aerial behavior can be expressed in a variety of ways, from subtle incomplete forms to complete and gloriously conspicuous *can't-miss-it* forms!

The supreme smoothness of dolphin skin further testifies to the streamlining forces of moving through water. Streamlining and smooth skin enables the dolphin to yield itself weightlessly to the sea. The exceptions are those fleeting occasions when it hurtles itself up into a bright world of distant horizons where its primary sense of echolocation is temporarily silenced and, for the moment of reentry, it may understand the bulk of its body.

Basic Clues

Yet, there are clues to why a dolphin is jumping. What aerial behavior does it use? Does it leave the water completely? Is anything stuck to the dolphin's body? Is the jumping dolphin alone or are there other dolphins present? If other dolphins are present, does the dolphin jump far from them or close to them? If it jumps close to them, does it also dive back in close to them? If so, how close? Dolphins can use the return dive for several reasons: to splash another dolphin in threat or invitation, warn it with a near-miss dive, or land on it in a direct hit. Finally, does one dolphin jump or do two or more dolphins jump at the same time?

More difficult to see, but highly informative, is the jumping dolphin's muscle tone when it jumps. How is the body held when the move is made? As in other mammals, flexible and fluid movements suggest play or good spirits. Stiff and rigid movements suggest aggression, anger, or fear.

PICTURE 11

*In this playful version of the **T-bone tactic**, Scarface slides smoothly and fluidly over Ski with a relaxed body. The T-bone tactic is the most "social" of the aerial behaviors at sea because it cannot occur without coordination between two dolphins. This aerial maneuver is used in a variety of social settings from play to combat, one reason why play is valuable practice should serious combat arise.*

CHAPTER 3

Why Dolphins Bow

PICTURE 12

*A **bow** is a high jump. A bow occurs when a dolphin jumps out of the water curled forward in the shape of a letter C to do a U-turn in the air and dive back close to the spot where it left the water (a body length or less). It is pronounced like the "bow" of a boat instead of "bow" and arrow.*

Dolphins bow for many different reasons, but sometimes also inadvertently provide extra information that is unrelated to the bow. Extra information includes the dolphin's gender, erections, pregnancy, and lactation as well as the pretty pink flush of an excited dolphin's genitals or chest. Bows can reveal a spotless, scar-free dolphin as well as a dolphin with a ghastly assortment of shark bite scars otherwise hidden below the water surface.

PICTURE 13
*Flash does a low or half bow called an **arched dive** and inadvertently reveals two grisly scars from shark bites.*

Bows are common among the dolphins of the "Enchanted River." They can be performed high in the sky or barely clear the water surface. No matter the variation, it is "Bow WOW!" for the lucky people who see or snap a picture of a bowing dolphin at sea. Dolphins bow for a remarkable variety of reasons.

PICTURE 14
*Before they became accustomed to being studied, some dolphins bowed next
to the boat repeatedly, as an early picture of Drake shows here. My impression is that he did this to get a better look at this unwelcome boat that followed him around. After a couple of these jumps, he decisively vanished.*

Bow: Are You FOLLOWING Me?

At the start of our study, the dolphins were unfamiliar to us and us to them. Florida dolphins are used to boats but not being followed by them for any length of time. Most of the dolphins took about two years before they accepted being studied, that is, before they habituated to our presence and grew accustomed to our frank interest in them.

Bow: Greeting after a Short Separation

On an early autumn survey of the study area, we had found Fran twice: first hunting alone with her son in the morning and second socializing with several other adults that afternoon. To that point in our study, Fran was a "skeptic," our term for a dolphin who fails to accept our presence even after years of exposure to us. Thus, in a surprise move as we approached the second encounter, she came directly over to the boat, did the full bow shown in Picture 15, and returned to her schoolmates. She did not have to make this obvious gesture. It was a first in our four-year acquaintance.

It took time to realize the significance of Fran's willowy bow because it took time to see that it marked a major change in her behavior: From then on she accepted us. It took her four years to do so, twice as long to habituate to us as most of the other dolphins. But it finally enabled us to study her at close range without disrupting her behavior. Thus, her sudden bow seemed to function as surprised recognition that we were part of the social landscape, evidence she then appeared to accept and continues to do as of this writing over a decade later.

PICTURE 15
A dolphin may jump close to the boat in recognition after a short separation. Here, Fran launches into a willowy bow the second time we saw her during a survey.

PICTURE 16

Dolphins may jump to greet a boat after a long absence. Here, Bruce bows at the boat twice with such suddenness that I barely managed to snare this shot of his second bow. We had not seen him for 6.5 months, but he knew us: By the day I took this picture, I had studied him 473 times.

Bow: Greeting after a Long Absence

Now that we have known many of the dolphins for years and we have seen each other hundreds of times, they bow close to the boat in greeting. The typical setting is when Capt. John and I find a familiar dolphin whom we have not seen for a long time because he or she had been absent from the study area. In these cases, their bows seem to function as unusually animated greetings.

Dolphins occasionally bow two or three times in a row. It is easy to miss the first one because the murky waters of the "Enchanted River" hide the dolphin until it breaks the surface. Waters are murky because soft sand and mud particles are easily disturbed and kept in suspension by fast-flowing currents. It is gratifying to have one's camera ready should the dolphin bow a second or third time.

Bow: Get a Better Look

The dolphin may compare the visual information available above the water, such as what the boat looks like, to the acoustic information available underwater, such as what the boat sounds like. If so, one wonders why they seek more information.

Sound is paramount to dolphins, but jumping to obtain visual information suggests the importance of vision to bottlenose dolphins. Considering that they are designed to live in murky water where visual information is typically limited, this is intriguing. What is the most important visual information under the sea?

PICTURE 17
Dolphins may bow close to the boat to get a better look. This is suggested by their tendency to jump to eye level, as Babyface shows here. The face-to-face view of the boat or people in the boat may be brief, but it probably provides a better view than peering up at the boat from down in the water while squinting against the sun.

Bow: Attract Attention

There are occasions, when we finish watching a dolphin and leave to continue the survey, that it suddenly starts jumping around. If this was the first time that the dolphin jumped during the observation, it is notable because it means that the dolphin jumped out of context with its previous activities. We return and watch some more. I do not know if our return is the jumping dolphin's intention. If it is, it works.

This setting usually involves a dolphin who is busy hunting as our boat idles nearby. The hungry dolphin is aware of our presence and of being observed but fails to acknowledge us in any way. Therefore, it may be a stretch to suggest that it suddenly starts jumping around as we leave *to regain our attention.* All one can say for sure is that their aerial activities are out of context with their previous activity, to which they return once we return and watch them some more.

For example, we watched young adult PeeWee hunting one soft spring day, putting a great deal of energy into pursuing fish the size of a person's little finger; they hardly seemed worth the effort she invested. When the time came to continue the survey, I kept watching PeeWee as Capt. John slowly pulled away. She suddenly did the memorable bow shown in Picture 18. It illustrates how she balances by extending her left pectoral fin yet appears to be waving. We came back and resumed watching her. She resumed hunting her tiny fish.

Intriguingly, PeeWee's mother has done the same thing several times: As we slowly leave after observing her, she suddenly starts doing aerial behaviors out of context with her previous activities. We return and watch some more. She resumes her previous activities.

PICTURE 18

A dolphin may jump to regain our attention. Here, PeeWee does a single bow and appears to be waving.

© 2004 Weaver

PICTURE 19

When I finally stood up, turned my back, and started to leave, the elephant suddenly began swaying and stamping, rattling her ears and the chain that bound her as best she could. Intrigued, I returned and resumed watching. She returned to her quiet sweeping and scooping.

Early in my career, I experienced the same thing when a captive elephant at the National Zoo suddenly began exhibiting exaggerated behaviors as I started to leave. Long an admirer of elephants, I had watched her rapt for many minutes as she used her trunk to sweep small wheat seeds into a neat pile, cup the pile carefully, scoop up several seeds with the tip of her trunk, and put them in her mouth with the delicacy of a person pressing a single sunflower seed between their lips. She did not eat all of her tiny wheat seeds at once, enabling her to repeat her sweeping-and-scooping series over and over and over. I realized that it was all she could do with her time, tethered as she was by the chain around her ankle that forced her to stand in one spot all day. (In conscientious zoos, such days of drudgery for elephants are over, while elsewhere many appalling "ecotourist" spots *torture* elephants so they pose for pictures with people.)

PICTURE 20
A young dolphin may jump to entice its mother to play. Here, Yukon (in the air) puts extra effort into his play invitation to his mom Yami (in the water) by doing a back bow. Like most mothers on land, mother dolphins at sea are too busy raising their young to play and make poor playmates as a rule. However, younger mothers are more playful than older mothers.

Like the dolphins at sea, the elephant had not indicated that she was aware of me or my rapt interest in her activities. But she obviously was, and it obviously mattered.

Bow: Entice Mother to Play

One steamy August day, young Yukon did not have any playmates his age. He was a yearling, the most playful time of life, so he invited his mom to play by bowing in her face repeatedly. He reminded me of a young monkey enticing another young monkey to play by bounding in front of it with a body suddenly made of rubber and dashing off in an obvious bid to be chased, and of Chrissie, my cat that invited me to play with her the same way.

Bow: Express Excitement over Novel Attention

Once they have weaned from their mothers to live independently, females on the "Enchanted River" take 4-6 years to grow up socially. That is, female sociosexual development is surprisingly extended. Young females are untried in the romantic arena, and many may jump to express excitement over the novelty of male attention. The aerial animation of such females usually involves a combination of several different maneuvers rather than a single type of jump.

PICTURE 21

*In this picture, 5-year-old Babyface is sent into aerial animation by un-usual attention from big bulls Drake and Bruce, unusual because they had focused their attentions on her mother Faye to this point in her young life. Babyface jumped with increasing vigor until her finale shown here, flinging herself backwards into the sea in a theatrical **back bow**.*

Bow: Encourage Desirable Suitors

PICTURE 22

*Even years after weaning, experienced females who are galvanized by qual-ity attention from particular males may jump to keep their attention. Here, Sylvia's **back bow** was part of the most spectacular display of athletic ardor in the romantic arena yet seen on the "Enchanted River." Sylvia performed so many amazing aerials that day, I could create an entire calendar!*

***

Bowing dolphins look like they are having fun or are at least in good spirits. Sometimes they are. Sometimes they are not. Like all mammals, dolphins have a range of emotions that includes irritation and anger. Considering that they are almost constantly in the company of other dolphins, they are remarkably peaceful. Irritation is rare.

But there are times when tensions arise, threats fly, and fights sometimes break out. Most tense exchanges are highly stylized and symbolic, with dolphins making rich use of choreographed behaviors like bows and other aerials. The following vignettes show the darker side of bows.

Bow: Discourage Unwanted Suitors

PICTURE 23

*A female dolphin may bow to avoid and warn bull dolphins to leave her alone. Here, Bette's sideways or **lateral bow** expresses her disinterest in the attention of two junior bulls. My interpretation of disinterest arose from before and after observations. Before the bow, the bulls followed Bette around. After the bow, they left. Bette's beautiful bow revealed the striking resemblance between dolphin and human belly buttons, and verified that she is a female.*

PICTURE 24

*Two dolphins perform back bows at the water surface called **lateral lurches**. This picture shows the two classic uses of this maneuver: a blind stab at penetration (lower dolphin) and avoiding penetration by rolling out of reach (upper dolphin).*

***

The next incidents describe the role of bows in escalating tensions among bulls.

PICTURE 25

Bulls may use aerial behaviors to spring out of the reach of rivals. Here, Vic uses a bow to catch his breath and avoid the bull coming up behind him. His move is similar to a young man, training to be a boxer, who dances around a stronger opponent to dodge his punches instead of punching him back. A very junior bull in this picture, Vic was easily intimidated and "jumpy" at the time. Some dolphins are jumpier than other dolphins, the way some people are jumpier than other people.

Bow: Dodge Play Punches

The social settings, as shown in Picture 25, involve mildly scuffling bulls. They do not appear to be in earnest because they tend to exchange soft strikes rather than hard punches and their exchanges do not accelerate into serious conflict. They are good practice.

Bow: Intimidate Rivals with Exaggeration

Bull dolphins employ many ways to establish their social rank among other bulls without risking injury from direct contact with them. As part of this political tool chest, bows can serve to display a dolphin's strength, speed, agility, and attitude.

In an episode involving four junior bulls wrestling to establish rank, two threatening bulls pushed and shoved two other bulls to intimidate them. Then they escalated their intimidation by employing aerial behavior.

In addition to wrestling and Fugazi's exaggerated bow in Picture 26 that day, the threatening junior bulls also used a heart-stopping high-speed game of "chicken" to intimidate the two other bulls. Recklessly, they zigzagged side-by-side through the razor-sharp oyster-laden pilings holding up a nearby dock in a clear demonstration of their agility and team spirit. They were so aroused, they even careened toward our boat and only veered away at the last second.

PICTURE 26
Very athletic bulls may exaggerate a bow to intimidate others. One of the threatening bulls, the athletic and spirited Fugazi, displays his strength by launching himself 12 feet into the sky. He displays his agility by diving at speed into water only ten feet deep yet dodging the sea floor looming up from below.

Whew! The moment impressed both Capt. John and I with a new respect for the speed, agility, and *intent* of battling bottlenose bulls.

Bow: Intimidate Rivals with a Symbolic Strike

During competition, a dolphin can do a carefully-aimed bow to dive back in so close to another dolphin that it serves as an intimidating near-miss threat. Bulls use this tactic more than the other age-sex classes. Consequently, bows used as near-miss threats were common during a prolonged phase of political unrest among nine bulls on the "Enchanted River" who formed a super-alliance that we call the Bowery Boys (Bruce, Drake, Nick, Rick, Reggie, Scrapefin Sam, Ski, Mike, and Lax). After the Bowery Boys successfully vanquished rivals from two neighboring super-alliances, the Punch Buddies and the Edge Alliance, they fought among themselves for the next two years. Their alliances shifted like sand in a wind storm as they established, broke, and renegotiated relationships and ranks among themselves. For example, "Rick the Restless" broke his current alliance, allied with Scrapefin Sam briefly, and broke that for an alliance with yet a third bull. That left Sam without an alliance partner.

PICTURE 27

Scrapefin Sam challenges Rick with a near-miss threat one cool December day against a backdrop of docks. Rick is in the water, barely visible by the tip of his ripped dorsal fin peaking out. Sam goes skyward to gain momentum and bows back in, barely missing Rick on the return dive. But that was his point. It was an example of how dolphins fight symbolically to avoid injury. Sam's bow also gave us a good look at the shark scars low on his tailstock.

On rare occasions, a dolphin may use a bow to intimidate a person the way they bow to intimidate another dolphin. A big bull we called Edge, for the dark rim on his dorsal fin, was also one of the edgiest bulls along our stretch of the "Enchanted River." Markedly intense, his irritable nature initiated more conflict among the dolphins than any other bull and even extended to kayakers. One afternoon, I was kayaking between mangrove isles where I had witnessed Edge and his bonded bull buddy harassing other dolphins that morning. Unexpectedly, Edge and his buddy were still there, now harassing junior bull Scrapefin Sam to the point of harrying him *out* of the water and up onto the sandbar to avoid them. I floated nearby, watching. Edge dove and reappeared suddenly over my head, bowing high in the sky above my kayak and glaring down. I saw for myself the true bulk of a bull dolphin's body, the bullying effect of a dolphin bowing overhead, and blunt forewarning in his glare. I instantly understood Sam's drastic measure of clambering onto the sandbar to avoid them!

Bow: Punch Rivals with Hard-hitting Intent

Dolphins are capable of poking and ramming each other with their hard mouths (rostrums). The small round bruises left behind on their bodies suggest that they poke each other with unsuspected regularity.

PICTURE 28

*Sometimes, symbolism is insufficient. When only a direct hit will do, a bull can bow out of the water to gain momentum to poke an opponent hard on his return dive, more intimidating than a mere threat to strike. Here, Scrapefin Sam does a low bow called an **arched dive** to gain traction to poke a younger opponent and establish his higher rank. Sam's arousal is obvious, although it was hard to tell if his erection was sexual or just general provocation. Dolphin sex is hard to see at sea.*

Bow: Aerial Combat

PICTURE 29

When tensions hit a fever pitch, dolphins fight. Fights also involve highly stylized maneuvers, as do less tense exchanges. The difference is that efforts to land a blow in a fight are sincere rather than symbolic. Here, a back bow turns into a head injury as two bulls collide.

PICTURE 30

Hard-hitting contact can bruise a dolphin seriously. Drake's brutal head bruise healed without a trace, but whether it damaged his echolocation abilities is unknown. Dolphins use echolocation to see with sound.

***

Bows can reveal important new information unrelated to the reason for the bow.

Bows: Reveal Pregnancy

PICTURE 31

A bowing dolphin can reveal that she is pregnant. This female suddenly bows in front of the boat for unknown reasons. Yet her gesture was enlightening because it revealed that she was pregnant. We cannot tell if a female dolphin swimming past the boat is pregnant because the water hides her underside.

PICTURE 32

A bowing dolphin can reveal that she is actively lactating and presumably still nursing her calf. Here, Sybil's lateral bow reveals her swollen mammaries. She sprang out of the water during a potential nursing dispute with her son Saga. The assumption of a nursing dispute was based on their entire exchange of ambiguous splashes and lunges.

Bows: Reveal Lactation

Mammaries filled with milk, as in Picture 32, reveal that mother dolphins of the "Enchanted River" may lactate until their calf is three years old. Calves start to hunt for fish when they are only a year old. They are hunting as actively as their mother when they are two years old. Thus, three years of lactation create a long overlap of living on milk and on solid foods. The overlap highlights the nutritional importance of milk and suggests that it takes 2-3 years for a calf to learn to hunt well enough to feed itself sufficiently. Finally, it illustrates the depth of investment mother dolphins put into raising their young.

Bow: Hide Information

PICTURE 33

The splashes of a bowing dolphin can also hide information. As Babyface demonstrates here, splashes often cover the genital field of the bowing dolphin and hide its gender. The splash serves as a seaside "fig leaf" like the literal fig leaves painted over the genitals of people in Renaissance oil paintings hung in fine art museums. Not shown is the frustration that such splashes engender in researchers, who have sometimes waited years to discover whether a dolphin is a male or a female!

Bow: Create an Illusion

PICTURE 34
Another way a bowing dolphin reveals information unrelated to its aerial maneuver occurs when it inadvertently creates an illusion. Here, the illusion is that the outer half of PeeWee's left pectoral fin appears to be bitten off. That is just an illusion created by the angle of her pectoral fin.

***

A clue about why dolphins jump is the number of dolphins who jump. One jumping dolphin is wonderful. Two jumping dolphins are spectacular.

Double Bows

A *double bow* occurs when two dolphins jump at the same time. They can be aimed in the same, different, or even opposite directions. Flashier versions of the double bow occur when the two dolphins aim at each other and crisscross in the sky. Double bows are rare on the "Enchanted River."

Double Bow: Reunion Greetings

The social setting of one showy episode of the double bow involved a small junior bull we call Plunder and a huge senior bull we call Simon. The small junior bull was ambling northward along the "Enchanted River." As he ambled abreast of the narrow opening to a side cove, the huge senior bull suddenly barreled out of it at him like a torpedo. The two met under water and then burst out of the sea together, as shown in Picture 35.

The senior bull far outranked the junior bull on the social ladder. There is little reason to expect the junior bull to defy the senior bull with any show of aggression or the senior bull to bother reinforcing his dominant status.

PICTURE 35

Dolphins may do a double bow in greeting. In this picture, the upper dolphin in the air is senior bull Simon. The lower dolphin coming out of the water is junior bull Plunder. They jump in tandem without touching and slide back into the water with barely a ripple.

They did this magnificent aerial maneuver twice and then traded places! Senior bull Simon headed out, ambling northward along the "Enchanted River" as Plunder had done. Junior bull Plunder entered the side cove out of which Simon had barreled and, finding a young bull like himself, stayed and played for an hour.

My interpretation was that Simon and Plunder's brief but highly charged exchange was a fleeting reunion. They knew each other well because they have a female in common, Plunder's mother. Simon is a dominant bull with an unusually devoted covey of females we call Simon's Sallies, and Plunder's mom is one of Simon's Sallies. As such, Simon is a good candidate for Plunder's father, though we assume that dolphin fathers do not know who their offspring are or a calf who its father is.

There are many examples of excited reunions like this. They include mothers and their grown calves (often with remarkable timing upon the birth of a new sibling), an older calf and his former babysitter, and adults. Reunions are often markedly affectionate. Our records sometimes show that the excited dolphins have not seen each other for a while although we can never be sure of that. Because dolphins greet each other so obviously and at times with conspicuous affection, I have come to believe that they greet our boat too.

Double Bow: Discourage Unwanted Females

PICTURE 36

Dolphins may do a double bow when one rejects the other. This picture shows the unexpected behavior of the bull warning away a female. Rick, the dolphin with his mouth open, threatens Sharon as she dives back in and eventually chases her away. Observations like this suggest that dolphins form real relationships based on likes and dislikes, as people do.

PICTURE 37

On rare occasions, several dolphins jump with choreographed precision.
One of these remarkable social settings, shown here, involved five bulls and
one female who engaged in such highly stylized, face-to-face swim patterns
that they resembled offensive and defensive football players facing one an-
other across a scrimmage line. Bruce, Drake, Ski, Reggie, and Scrapefin
Sam apparently used the stylized moves to compete over the sole female.
For her part, Sylvia matched the moves of Bruce and Drake. By matching
their moves, in essence dancing with them, she may have revealed her pref-
erences for them over the other would-be suitors.

Quadruple Bow: Choreographed Rivalry

The dolphins of the "Enchanted River" exhibit a variety of rhythmic swim patterns and aerial behaviors that involve multiple dolphins who clearly coordinate their moves with one another. The clear choreography of these patterns is one of the reasons I think that matching movements and synchrony play a large role in the art of dolphin communication.

***

There is another type of double bow performed by dolphins on the "Enchanted River" called the *T-bone tactic.* The most common of the double bows, these showy behaviors are used in so many ways that they warrant their own chapter.

CHAPTER *4*

Why Dolphins Use T-bone Tactics

A breathtaking version of a double bow, the *T-bone tactic* occurs when two airborne dolphins align perpendicular to each other and fleetingly form the shape of the letter T, hence the term T-bone. The upper dolphin bows high in the sky over the lower dolphin. The lower dolphin lunges out of the water to ram or pretend to ram the upper dolphin. This handy maneuver has many variations, may or may not include direct physical contact, and occurs in many social settings ranging from play to pain.

PICTURE 38
Cheerful versions of the T-bone tactic occur during good-natured wrestling matches. In this picture, the two bulls are playing but probably also probing each other's physical skills and willingness to cooperate in coordinated maneuvers. The lower dolphin emerging from the water, burly bull Ski, barely taps the upper dolphin, Scarface, whose brief balancing act reveals his male gender.

T-bone: Pure Play

PICTURE 39

Calves use the T-bone tactic in pure play. This suggests that dolphins are given to lunging and dodging lunges from an early age. A close look at this sunny photo reveals a tiny remora clinging near the belly button of the upper dolphin, Amy.

T-bone: Self-handicapping in the Name of Play

PICTURE 40

Nick uses a T-bone tactic during gentle play with young calf Celine one dark winter day as her mother hunts nearby. The calf Celine is the upper dolphin. Nick is the lower dolphin. As a bulky bull, he holds back the potential power of his lunge, self-handicapping in the name of play. Most bulls of the "Enchanted River" are playful and affectionate with calves.

T-bone: Pestering Mother

Dolphin kids are like other kids: They pester their mothers. Dolphin mothers are like other mothers: They tolerate their child's pestering for a time but eventually become annoyed and chastise the calf by lunging at it. Such lunges are usually mild at best, mere symbolic warnings like one person only pretending to slap another person. Mothers and calves create the T-bone tactic together when mom lunges at calf and calf dodges her by springing into the air.

PICTURE 41

Mothers use the T-bone tactic to discipline their calves. In this picture, young Yukon pesters his mother to play. Finally fed up, his young mother Yami launches out of the water in a mock threat to T-bone him. He avoids her by bouncing in the air with extra spring in his step.

Alas, her lunge does not deter him. Yukon continues to jump at his mom, each jump fancier than before. In response, mom Yami launches at him further and further out of the water.

PICTURE 42
Finally, Yami launches nearly out of the water yet still barely clips her son.
Done loosely without hard-hitting smacks, mother and son's fanciful demon-
strations of the classic T-bone tactic suggest a combination of play, teasing
youthful rebellion, and mild maternal discipline.

T-bone: Slipping a Schoolmate a Slap

PICTURE 43
A dolphin can use the T-bone to slip a schoolmate a teasing slap. Here,
jostling calves demonstrate how the T-bone tactic is easily revised into
a handy maneuver for tapping a playmate on the head with one's flukes.
This gesture, of course, exposes the tapping dolphin to a retaliatory poke
on the belly!

T-bone: Getting to Know You

PICTURE 44

Young male Laska leaps over big Bowery Boy bulls Mike and Lax in a constrained version of the T-bone. This picture demonstrates one of the many social complexities among the dolphins of the "Enchanted River," in this case the fact that big bulls are more likely to socialize with male calves than with female calves.

PICTURE 45

A common use of the T-bone tactic involves a shy young female who springs into the sky to avoid male attention. In this picture, the upper dolphin is teen female Amy. The two lower dolphins who followed her halfway out of the water in a unison spyhop are bulls Scrapefin Sam and Ski. Amy jumps to dodge them yet remains nearby instead of swimming away swiftly, contradictory gestures that reveal her ambivalence. Young and untried, Amy keeps bouncing around and the bulls' interest in her quickly wanes.

It seems to me that the bulls' notable preference for male over female calves could be related to construction of the bulls' complex social networks - *if* bulls begin building relationships with male calves still young enough to be dependent on their mothers. Perhaps it is never too early to recruit a future alliance partner in this long-lived political species.

T-bone: Bashful about Bulls

Female dolphins on the "Enchanted River" do not become pregnant with their first calf until they are 8-12 years old. Theirs is a long adolescence in the animal kingdom, the initial stages of which they spend adjusting to bull attention. It is a standard part of bottlenose dolphin female social development at sea to be bashful about bulls.

Many aerials do double duty. In Picture 45, Amy's high bow verified her gender as a female. It also revealed the wincing reality of a shark bite scar in the crotch, visible when zooming in on the picture with computer software. Surprisingly, the bite did not interfere with her future reproductive life.

***

The above episodes show that some T-bone tactics are used in light-hearted social settings. However, most occur because the dolphin leaping into the air is trying very hard to avoid the dolphin who lunges after it out of the water.

PICTURE 46
Finally fed up, Nick launches himself at Sybil in a T-bone tactic. Here, she bounces skyward to avoid him. His pointed gesture reminds everybody of his competitive intent. Of note, Nick lunged at Sybil instead of at her suitors.

T-bone: Avoiding Annoyed Suitors

Courtship can get testy. A bull can use the T-bone tactic to express his irritation with a female he is courting. In the spring and summer of 2009, male rivalry for Sybil hit fever pitch. She roamed around the "Enchanted River" hounded by suitors. As the escort bull, beefy Nick stayed staunchly at her side. But they were stalked by several more suitors, each poised to pounce on any opportunity. Sybil's increasing fertility forced the rivals into ever-closer company. Tensions simmered like heated water.

One day, Sybil went into a small cove to search for food. Her suitors followed her in dutifully. Hunting dolphins work independently, each to find his or her own fish. Accordingly, they all spread out across the little cove. When Nick left Sybil to hunt, another suitor immediately took his place at her side. This forced Nick to rush back to her to protect his status as the escort bull. Nick's hunt was interrupted like this several times.

T-bone: Avoiding Annoying Suitors

Irritation in the romantic arena goes both ways. Females on the "Enchanted River" can choose to accept or reject male attention. They usually reject it by leaving or threatening unwanted suitors rather than challenging them directly. Although it is a drastic measure, a well-placed T-bone tactic helps the female avoid unwanted suitors as she expresses her disinterest.

Sometimes direct messages are required, whereupon the lower dolphin tries to ram the upper dolphin rather than just pretending or threatening to ram it. One summer evening, a junior

PICTURE 47
Here, in another version of the T-bone tactic, pregnant PeeWee springs out of the water to avoid burly bull Ski. Just four months into a 12-month pregnancy, PeeWee uses acrobatic expressions of avoidance. In contrast, heavily pregnant females in late term tend to warn bulls away with threatening arched dives or tail slaps rather than more athletic communiqués.

bull pestered several adult females for attention. They tolerated his efforts for a while and then started lunging at him, forcing him to leap into the sky to avoid their irritated pokes and prods. Creating T-bone silhouettes against the orange and pink pastels of sunset, his plight looked poetic to nearby cheering boaters.

T-bone: Bickering over Babies

Maturing females on the "Enchanted River" show increasing interest in other females' calves, nature's way of preparing them for motherhood. However, learning how to be a good mother at sea is challenging when the calf's mother vetoes a maturing female's interest in her baby. In these settings, the T-bone tactic is a useful device for communicating one's intentions, although other aerial behaviors are often called into play as well.

When PeeWee was five months into her first pregnancy, two mother dolphins vetoed her interest in their babies, but PeeWee failed to respect their wishes. This episode was extraordinary because of its rarity: The three females went on to argue with aerial behaviors like fighter pilots in a World War II dog fight among the clouds. Fighting in the water, the dolphins made liberal use of the T-bone tactic.

It started when PeeWee began playing with two calves whose mothers were hunting nearby. One of the mothers came over and ushered the calves away, halting play abruptly. This is standard maternal behavior by a mother dolphin who does not approve of her calf's playmate.

The abandoned playmate seldom disputes this protective maternal maneuver. But, apparently frustrated, PeeWee did not take 'no' for an answer. First, she did a series of bows. Pretty to watch, the bows nonetheless probably vented her frustration and served as warnings to the mothers, for she returned and started playing with the calves again.

PICTURE 48
As PeeWee returns to the calves, one of the protective mothers races over and, with a determined T-bone, pecks her hard enough to create a fleeting dent in her skin. PeeWee jumps to avoid the protective mother but not high enough.

PeeWee retaliated with a looming round of threats to body slam each mother in turn. However, her threats were symbolic. She did not actually body slam either mother. Instead, she used near-miss aerial maneuvers as in Picture 49 to merely pelt each mother with big menacing splashes.

Having made her point, PeeWee left. PeeWee was clearly excited this day and jumped 8 times altogether. It is interesting to speculate about her reasons beyond denied desires to play. For example, some dolphins are more "jumpy" than other dolphins – more likely to express

PICTURE 49
PeeWee drops down in a resolute belly breach and pelts one of the protective mothers with big menacing splashes.

PICTURE 50
PeeWee bullies the other protective mother by doing a side bow over her and landing a moment later, sending a menacing cascade of splashes over the other mother dolphin who denied her desire to play with the calves.

themselves with aerial maneuvers – the way some people are more likely to dance than other people. PeeWee is a "jumpy" dolphin. In addition, she was pregnant. Her hormones conceivably prodded her actions to unusual heights. On the other hand, PeeWee may have been pulling social rank on the mothers. PeeWee's mother is a regal dolphin we eventually nicknamed Queen Priscilla for her imperious attitude about other dolphins. Maybe "Princess PeeWee" felt justified in throwing a little tantrum because she thought that she out-ranked the protective mothers who denied her desires to play with their calves.

***

When Tensions Run High and Restraint Runs Low

We see few dolphin fights on the "Enchanted River." Most are arguments conducted with *symbolic* aerial behaviors. This is notable because symbolic gestures require *restraint*. In contrast, recall from the use of bows in combat that dolphins can and do body slam each other in serious fights (Pictures 28-30). They can cause considerable injury, and even kill another dolphin by knocking it unconscious or ramming its vital organs. The following vignettes show how the T-bone tactic is used when tensions run high and restraint runs low.

T-bone: Harrying

PICTURE 51

Here, senior bull Nick harries junior bull Puck with a T-bone tactic during a prolonged exchange that effectively prevents Puck's access to nearby fertile female Queen Priscilla. A worthy competitor, Puck volleys with the bigger bull for many minutes. But Nick's pugnacious intolerance of the junior bull's presence near a fertile female translates into increasingly harder collisions that eventually provoke Puck into flight. In this picture, Puck avoids Nick by springing into the air but lands on him squarely in the water before sprinting away. Nick follows Puck for half a mile, where the skirmish continues.

T-bone: Testing

PICTURE 52

Here, the T-bone tactic involves a hard hit above the water surface. Scarface (lower dolphin) lunges vigorously at Trix (upper dolphin), who falls on him backwards with a sturdy strike. Such exchanges provide valuable lessons on one's own strength and endurance as well as those of schoolmates. Direct hits like this tend to be silent rather than sound like a loud slap, perhaps because the dolphins are wet.

T-bone: Stylized Combative Exchange

PICTURE 53

Resident bull Drake lunges at visiting bull Newton with aggressive intent. Newton dodges Drake by spyhopping high into the sky and prepares to fall backwards onto his lunging opponent. This is one of several different ways to create the T in a T-bone tactic, in this case varying the usual bow performed by the upper dolphin. This conflict was prolonged as Drake takes unusually hostile exception to Newton's uncommon presence.

***

T-bone: Mother's Determined Discipline

PICTURE 54
*Dolphin mothers are generally patient. Yet on occasion, they too become
sufficiently annoyed with their calves to give them a hard poke instead of
just threatening to do so. Here, Courtney launches out of the water and
disciplines her daughter, Cutlass, for disobedience with a hard poke in the
side. Cutlass leaps to avoid her mother, though not high enough.*

This social setting involved our boat. Courtney and Cutlass were inside on the Intracoastal
Waterway heading for The Pass to go outside into the Gulf of Mexico. When we approached
them, the mother dolphin Courtney kept going but her daughter Cutlass swung over to us instead and dallied, dancing around our boat. Courtney tolerated this for several minutes, twice
returning to fetch her daughter and resume their steady course towards the Gulf. Cutlass kept
dallying at our boat.

Finally goaded, Courtney zipped back a third time and gave her errant daughter the hard
poke shown in Picture 54. After that, Cutlass swam obediently at her mother's side as they left
together. Such episodes suggest that maritime mothers expect their calves to comply with their
wishes when they communicate their desired direction and speed.

T-bone: Pestering an Aged Lady

The T-bone tactic is stylized and therefore easy to recognize. However, the reason it occurs can
be hard to understand.

Many uses of the T-bone tactic only *symbolize* a threat and reveal that dolphin communication is often indirect. They remind me of arguing people who only pretend to slap each other.
There is nothing imaginary about the aerial behaviors in the next chapter.

PICTURE 55

Rare use of the T-bone tactic involves a teen female pestering an older female. One winter day, young Sylvia teased gentle old Tess in a sheltered bay. Tess finally reared out of the water in reprisal. As shown here, her weak lunge was symbolic at best, but sufficient reprisal to send her young provocateur Sylvia leaping into the air. Why young Sylvia pestered Tess remains a mystery.

CHAPTER 5

Why Dolphins Breach

A *breach* is a body slap. A breach occurs when a dolphin shoots out of the water and drops flatly onto the water surface the way a falling tree drops flatly onto the ground. The flat landing distinguishes breaches from other aerial behaviors, creating big splashes and lots of noise.

PICTURE 56
*This picture shows the moment of impact from Scrapefin Sam's back breach. Because Sam landed flatly on his back, his aerial behavior is called a **back breach**.*

PICTURE 57
IMPACT!! This picture shows the big splashes that breaching dolphins create when they land.

A breaching dolphin may or may not leave the water completely. But the breaching dolphin who does leave the water completely hits it harder upon its return and makes a bigger splash. Either way, remember "Breach ***BOOM!"***

The breach is named for the body part that hits the water. A dolphin who lands flatly on its stomach is doing a *belly or ventral breach*, on its side is doing a *side* or *lateral breach*, and on its back an *inverted or back breach*. Breaches are less common than bows and T-bone tactics but are more common than leaps among the dolphins of the "Enchanted River."

Dolphins on the "Enchanted River" breach when they are aggravated.

PICTURE 58
Illustration of a humpback whale in mid-air during a lateral breach. Breaching is standard behavior for many cetaceans. In Baja's Gulf of California, I saw humpback, sperm, and fin whales breach but did not see blue or Brydes whales breach.

Breach: Remove Annoying Hitchhikers

PICTURE 59

Here, Fennel's bow reveals a remora clinging to her stomach. Remoras are cleaner fish that scour the sensitive dolphin skin looking for tidbits. They are similar to the algae-eater fish that roam the glass walls of our aquarium looking for algae to eat. Remoras clean many sea creatures as they feed, including turtles and whale sharks.

Remoras are the main reason why calves breach. Nothing agitates a dolphin calf more than these antagonizing hitchhikers. Judging from a calf's frenzied reactions to one or more remoras scouring its body, remoras hurt.

PICTURE 60

This is an overhead picture of a remora that shows the oblong suction cup on the top of its head. The suction cup is made of plates that are lined with holdfasts called spinules that clench by piercing delicate dolphin skin with countless pin-pricks. It is one of nature's most extraordinary modifications of a dorsal fin.

Because hairless human skin is sensitive, any unwelcome creature crawling on us, like a spider, automatically triggers removal efforts. Luckily, most crawling creatures do not cling and are easily brushed off with an effortless swipe of a hand. Hairless dolphin skin is sensitive too, but because remoras cling and dolphins lack hands, a dolphin cannot brush off a remora with an effortless swipe of its hand. Whenever I watch a young dolphin flaying frantically but futilely to remove a remora, I consciously value my hands.

PICTURE 61
A finger-long remora clenches Prism's belly button. Regardless of their size, remoras drive calves crazy.

PICTURE 62
Vic twists wildly and then breaches to remove the tiny remora clenching his stomach. Small dolphins who twist wildly in the air like this and land flatly on the water are learning to breach to remove their antagonizing hitchhiker.

PICTURE 63

Remora removal is not instinctive and must be learned. Here, PeeWee breaches on her back although the remora clings to her stomach. Remoras harass calves more than older dolphins. This is probably because older dolphins have learned to remove remoras with a well-placed body slam.

PICTURE 64

*Nine-month-old PeeWee gives the most energetic demonstration of aerial behaviors in **remora
removal** yet seen on the "Enchanted River." Tormented, she bowed and breached 100 times in a row
trying to remove her remora. These pictures are only a glimpse of her struggles. PeeWee may look
like she is expressing the joy of life or joi de vivre but is not. She is in anguish.*

PICTURE 65

As Cutlass demonstrates here, the best way to remove a remora is to strike the water hard and fast by breaching.

Breach: Play

On occasion, breaching calves are playing.

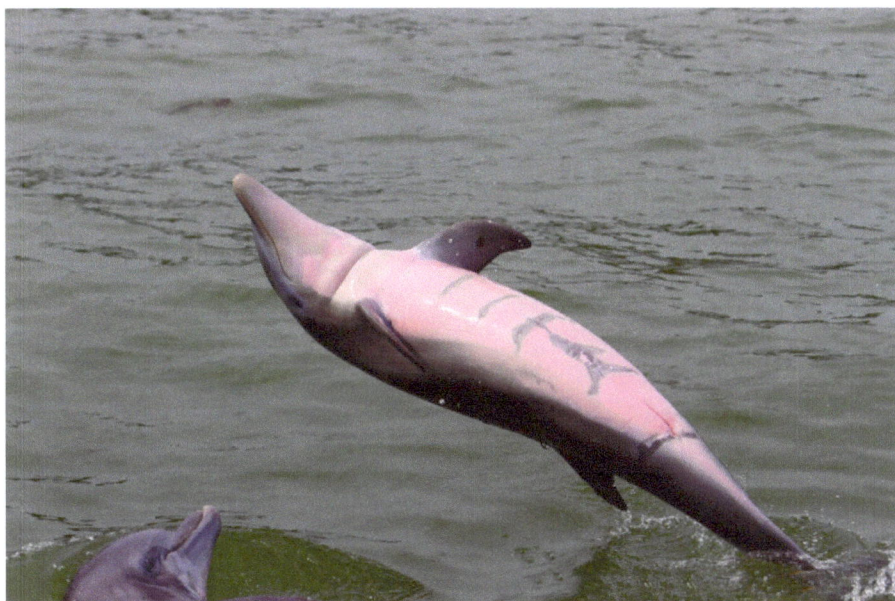

PICTURE 66

*Late afternoon one summer day, yearling Sahara shoots out of the water in a **back breach** while playing with her 4-year-old sibling Saltan and 3-year-old playmate Astor. Her breach reveals an unsuspected element of dolphin healing: Flushing from the excitement of play, her belly is pink yet her scars are gray. How Sahara became scarred is unknown, but the even spacing of her scar pattern suggests that her stomach was slit open by the propellers of a passing boat, and that she dodged death.*

PICTURE 67

*Even in play, schoolmates must keep a sharp lookout. Animated by her
caper with young teens in this picture, Sahara has launched another breach
to land on Astor lying just under the surface. Ka-BOOM!*

Adult dolphins also breach when they are annoyed. Annoyance occurs in two main
settings: annoyance with boats and annoyance with other dolphins.

Breach: Annoyed by Boats

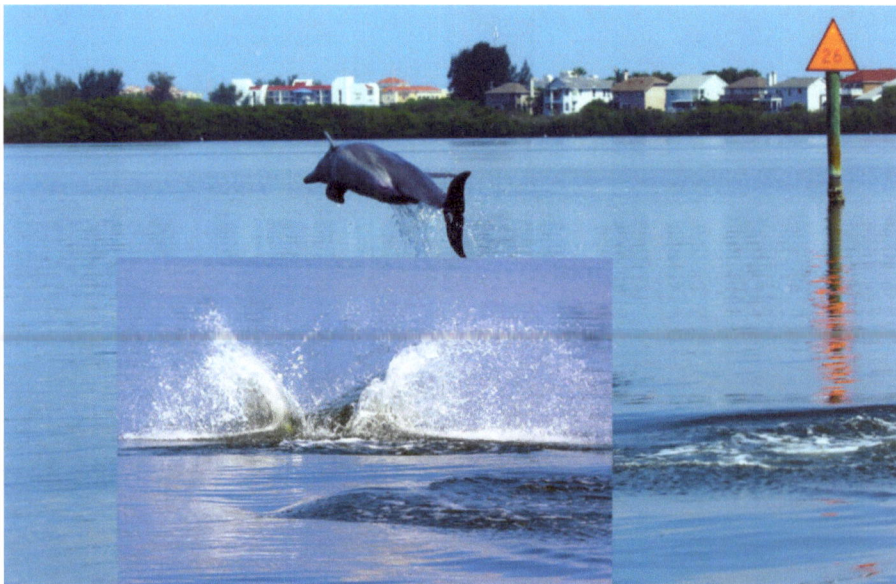

PICTURE 68

*Rick breaches on a brilliant blue day to clearly communicate that our pres-
ence is unwelcome. A breach is a strong message of irritation, particularly
among lone dolphins who have been followed by watercraft too closely or for
too long. When a dolphin breaches, the boat captain puts the boat in neutral
gear, and the dolphin vanishes, it is safe to say that the dolphin was annoyed
with the boat. Weak signs of annoyance are tail slaps (although not necessarily) and subtle signs include zigzag swimming and other evasive efforts.*

Breach: Vent Frustration with the Mating Game

PICTURE 69

Bulls may breach when their bids for female attention are rejected. One summer day, Scrapefin Sam is searching for a bite to eat in a deep hole in the seafloor near an outcropping of seaside homes as Clara passes through. She alters her course and swings over to Sam in greeting. He swims to her side immediately, but she keeps going without pause. Apparently rejected, his reaction is to fly extra high into the sky and drop down in a booming breach as she left. She did not return.

I wonder if some breaches are like a person pounding a table with their fist: It vents frustration; however, it hurts too. The rejected bull dolphin who breaches may go on to perform additional aerial behaviors that are less hard-hitting.

***

Mysterious Breaches

There are occasions when a dolphin does a series of hard-hitting breaches for reasons I cannot fathom. These mysterious breaches occur in social settings that have little in common. Moreover, the reactions of schoolmates vary. Some schoolmates come over, suggesting that a series of breaches is an attention-getting invitation. Others do not react visibly, a lack of response that is particularly striking when the breach series is almost conducted on top of them. Schoolmates may be reacting vocally instead of visibly; alas, we are not privy to this precious information because we cannot hear dolphins vocalize from our moving boat.

Mysterious Breaches: Wiggling Readjustments?

Some pregnant dolphins breach many times in a row for unknown reasons. One mid-May day, heavily-pregnant Xanadu was meandering sleepily among scattered schoolmates when, without warning, she suddenly heaved her thick body into 18 breaches in a row! She tired quickly, however, launching well out of the water on her first breaches but less than half way out on her final breaches. Two new bulls joined her after she finished, so her mysterious display may have been an invitation or they just came over to see what was going on.

PICTURE 70

*Heavily-pregnant Xanadu slams her right side against the water surface and raises her left pectoral fin in a **lateral breach**. Her splash illustrates how hard a breaching dolphin may hit the water despite launching only half way out.*

Five days after Xanadu's breach series, another heavily-pregnant female exhibited a similar series of breaches. Across the years, intermittent observations of heavily-pregnant females who suddenly perform a breach series or roll around the water surface snapping at drifting vegetation raise questions about the potential discomfort of pregnancy. Do pregnant dolphins use aerial behaviors to shift their big babies into a different position? Are they reacting to its movements?

Mysterious Breaches: Excited by Social Circumstances?

PICTURE 71
Another mysterious series of 11 breaches occurred between two exciting so-cial events that may have invigorated the performer, Yami, to reach unusual heights. Here, she watches me take her picture as she winds up for another one of her many breaches.

The first exciting social event was an obvious greeting by two groups of dolphins who changed course to join directly, circle around one another like a swift merry-go-round, and then continue on their separate ways. If they had been people, we might think it was a chance meeting of members of two college cliques with great affection for each other but beholden to different, tight schedules.

The second exciting event was a vast convergence of 19 dolphins in a magical maritime event I call an "Out of the Blue." In this behavior, more and more dolphins appear from 'out of the blue' and gather together. These events are magical for me because the more dolphins, the better. Even more magical, we are awarded the privileged status of traveling alongside as they amble about in loose parade formation. The closeness of so many wild dolphins, the gliding rhythm of their pace, their whispering breaths, and prolonged exposure is time travel back to Eden when Man and Animal were friends.

Yami did her breach series between these two exciting events. Swimming steadily from the affectionate greeting to the assembling "Out of the Blue" parade with her young son Yukon and Babyface, Yami executed her breach series with great skill, landing precisely between Babyface and young Yukon without brushing them. For their part, Yukon and Babyface stayed their course without obvious reaction. Yami completed each breach with the same energy and bounce without tiring, like a young dancer. Yet her pirouettes were hard-hitting. There was more to her behavior than the poetry of motion, but I never figured out what it was.

Mysterious Breaches: Warning Sea Creatures Away?

PICTURE 72

*One windy day, Scrapefin Sam breaches 11 times in a row. The large photo
shows one of the big splashes from his breaches. The small inset photo
shows how he twists wildly in the air before landing.*

In addition to breaching, Sam smacked his head on the water surface repeatedly. He reminded me of the way a newly-wounded dolphin writhes in pain at the water surface, though we did not see any obvious wound on him. Nor did we see a remora on him. Finally, his behavior was out of context with the behavior of other dolphins socializing nearby.

Sam's behavior suggests that a dolphin **might** repeatedly breach to warn another sea creature away. Two thought-provoking photos show Sam landing on what appears to be a second fin that, from its angle, could not have belonged to him. I have not reproduced these photos here because the details are fuzzy. None the less, they raise the possibility that Sam was breaching on or near a shark to warn it that it has been spotted and best leave, the way an African gazelle leaps repeatedly to notify a lurking leopard that it has been spotted and best leave. For more suggestive evidence that dolphins use aerial behaviors to warn another sea creature away, see Chapter 7 on using tail slaps to warn away a shark.

***

Bows and breaches are maritime high jumps. The aerial behaviors in the next chapter are maritime long jumps.

CHAPTER 6

Why Dolphins Leap

PICTURE 73
*A **leap** is a long jump. A leap occurs when a dolphin clears the water and, fully stretched out from head to flukes, covers the length of its own body over the water surface at a minimum before diving back in. Leaps are the least common aerial behavior among the dolphins of the "Enchanted River."*

Dolphins leap when they need speed. They leap to arrive somewhere or leave somewhere *fast*. Dolphin skin is designed to glide through water smoothly, but it still experiences some friction. A leaping dolphin swims more efficiently because water friction is removed for the moment the dolphin is airborne. Local dolphins tend to leap suddenly and usually in the distance far from the boat, qualities that make it hard to obtain focused photos.

One dolphin in a group may leap, or the entire group may leap. A dolphin may leap once, or it may leap several times in a row. Leaping several times in a row is behavior called *porpoising*. Porpoising dolphins are marvelous to see; check the internet for magnificent videos of vast herds of porpoising dolphins. I saw countless herds of porpoising dolphins offshore of Baja. Porpoising typically occurs offshore and I have yet to see coastal dolphins porpoising down the "Enchanted River."

Instead, leaping occurs in two typical scenarios locally. One is a dolphin rushing past at great speed, visible during one or two memorable leaps but otherwise hidden during long stretches of rapid underwater travel. Most vanish and take their reasons for rushing with them. However, we have been able to solve these mysteries of leaping occasionally.

Leap: Racing to a Rendezvous

For example, leaping dolphins may be racing to a rendezvous with other dolphins. One summer day, Lana and her son Laska leapt out of the water in the distance and vanished. Underwater and unseen, they raced to the bridge in the middle of our study area where they leapt once again, enabling us to track them.

On the other side of the bridge, Lana and Laska joined several more mother-calf pairs swirling in great excitement around two tiny, shiny newborn dolphins. In the next hour, several more dolphins joined the excited group from all points to visit the new moms. Dolphins are attracted to newborns, as are monkeys, apes, people, and elephants.

Leap: Fleeing Sharks

PICTURE 74

Dolphins may leap to flee from a shark. We have only witnessed one confirmed shark flight on the "Enchanted River" involving the yearling calf Saga. He was bitten 9 times in that sole episode, but he survived. This is a picture of three of his scars a year later. The two upright crescents show where the shark bit over Saga's back. The upside-down crescent shows where the shark bit over Saga's stomach.

Leap: Fleeing Suitors

PICTURE 75

Most teen females have mixed feelings about male attention and may leap to flee from amorous bulls. This picture of young Sharon blasting past our boat shows how she strains to gain speed. She ducks over to us and weaves under our bow, asking us to accelerate so she can surf our boat as a get-away car. We fail to react instantly and she resumes her wild sprint across the seas.

It was soon obvious why Sharon strained to gain speed: to escape the cadre of breathless suitors who chased her. The bulls pursued her past our boat and eventually caught up to her, but then fought among themselves with a single-mindedness that allowed Sharon to slip away.

***

The other typical scenario, and more likely to occur locally, is a dolphin leaping through a group of dolphins to gain their attention. This has numerous applications on the "Enchanted River."

Leap: Seeking Attention

A female may leap through a group to gain their attention. Midway through her first pregnancy, PeeWee flitted through her social group, trying to socialize with each dolphin in turn. PeeWee swam briefly with her mother, Queen Priscilla, who left PeeWee abruptly to return to her hunt. Then PeeWee started to play with her little brother Prism, but Queen P returned and took little brother away with her. Finally, PeeWee tried to visit Babyface and the bulls, but they were too preoccupied with one another to respond to her. Everyone was busy.

PICTURE 76

Finding all of her schoolmate busy, PeeWee does her unexpected, high fly-ing leap through the group shown here, signals them with a splashy return dive, and vanishes.

A male may leap through a group of dolphins to gain their attention, too. One standard scenario involves two bonded bulls traveling with a female. One bull swims at the female's side as the escort bull. This relegates his alliance partner to the social sidelines. Marginalized, the so-called peripheral bull often leaps about with atypical animation as if trying to draw the female's attention.

As it turns out, bulls on the "Enchanted River" leap through a group of dolphins to gain attention in a striking variety of scenarios. Most of these striking scenarios involve other bulls.

***

Leaping takes muscle. It means arousal. Leaping dolphins have been provoked. Some of the most provocative settings involve establishing one's social status. Social status is crucial to bulls in particular because rank dictates their quality of life and potentially the quality of their mates. Across his lifetime, a bull must establish himself with each bull in a changing procession of bulls. Some of his relationships will be stable. Many others will be unstable and demand continual testing, as younger bulls strengthen and older bulls weaken. The web of social rela-tionships that emerges among bottlenose dolphin bulls is dynamic and complex enough to be called political. I call their web the *bottlenose bullpen* or just the *bullpen*.

The cornerstone of the bullpen on the "Enchanted River" is leaping. Because leaping is used to challenge rivals for social status, leaps and their corollaries, skims, play political center stage.

A *skim* is a type of leap in which the dolphin slices through the interface between air and water, sending rooster tail splashes off both sides of its body. In a *unison skim,* two dolphins skim together at the same time side by side. Like bows and breaches, leaps and skims are very showy behaviors.

Leap: Challenging Rivals in the Bullpen

PICTURE 77

*A bull may leap through a dolphin group to challenge his rivals. Here, junior bull Oliver skims past a group of dolphins one winter day as part of a brassy confrontation of leaps and skims to challenge senior bulls. Oliver's brazen **barreling bull display** is the maritime counterpart to a younger blackback gorilla beating his chest on the sidelines of an older silverback gorilla's harem to challenge the harem master and to entice a female to leave the harem and join him.*

Nick and Rick had been hunting along a seawall with fertile female Sybil when Oliver blasted past them, skimming through the surface at top speed in a conspicuous and unexpected 'barreling bull display.' Fertile female forgotten, senior bulls Nick and Rick shot after the challenger. Maintaining his speed, young Oliver sprinted the half mile to the other end of the bay. We tracked him by his skims. The senior bulls galloped after him but did not, or could not, catch him. Oliver circled around and sprinted all the way back to the starting point of his display, as displaying bulls often do. In total he sprinted nearly a mile, surely a display of superior stamina in a species that swims without ceasing.

Oliver's bold challenge also opened the door for a display of psychological stamina. While pursued by the senior bulls, he took a wrong turn and headed down an aquatic blind alley between fingers of land created for seaside homes. The senior bulls pounced on the opportunity and cornered him in the cul-de-sac. They blocked his exit for many minutes before allowing him to creep out cautiously along the seawalls to freedom.

I don't know who won that round between Nick, Rick, and young Oliver, but Oliver left the area; we did not see him for the next year. When he returned, the three bulls resumed displaying for each other. This led to further examples of the political applications of aerial behaviors at sea (Picture 161).

Leap: Long Chases to Escape the Bullpen

Not all competing dolphins who leap through the bullpen circle back for more. Many leap in one direction: out! Should rivals chase and catch them, brawls often break out.

One winter competition like this involved two pairs of alliance partners who brawled between three long-distance chases in which leaping played a central role. In total, junior bulls W.R. and Gazio sprinted across two miles of water, and senior bulls Scrapefin Sam and Ski chased them the entire distance. Such athletic episodes display physical stamina as well as the efforts that bottlenose bulls invest in their social status. The lesser-ranked of the two pairs, W.R. and Gazio, had started the sprinting.

PICTURE 78

Although a champion sprinter, junior bull W.R. fled a confrontation by leaping across the sea but was chased and caught by senior bull Ski. Here, W.R. lunges out of the water to avoid being toothraked by Ski's sharp teeth. Between lunging and leaping, brawling bulls use whatever aerial behaviors they need.

Two years later, W.R. and Gazio were embroiled in another bullpen competition and again sprinted away. Sprinting had become their signature combat style. They usually used it to avoid aggression from higher-ranking bulls but for darker deeds as well, once sprinting all the way across a bay to antagonize a mother and her young calf.

Leap: Short Chases around the Bullpen

PICTURE 79
A dolphin may leap during a short chase. In this picture, a junior bull evades a rival junior bull against dramatic summer skies. Chases are uncommon on the "Enchanted River" and tend to be short. In this chase, the fleeing bull swam in a small circle and came right back for more.

The two bulls in Picture 79 scuffled with several other junior bulls at length. Their gripping competitions drew a crowd of human and dolphin onlookers, a revealing reflection of how, like people, bottlenose dolphins pay attention to one another's social lives. The dolphin onlookers included a number of senior bulls who milled nearby, monitoring the brawls without joining the competition. Such behavior intrigues me because it suggests how bull dolphins gain important information about social ranks through observation only.

Leap: Unison Skims to Test the Bullpen

Bonded bull buddies advertise their team spirit by performing the same behavior at the same time side by side, that is, by synchronizing. By performing a synchronized version of the skimming behavior that Oliver used to challenge senior bulls Nick and Rick (Picture 77), bonded bull buddies can enhance their display even more by performing skims in unison.

The unison skim is an argumentative gesture. It always looks the same: That is, it is highly stylized. Bulls seem to use this gesture to be seen rather than directly engaged, rather like shouting and clenching a fist at people down on the sidewalk from a second story window. I am not sure if the performing bulls use it in order to elicit a direct response but, in any case, a unison skim is rarely followed by obvious retaliatory gestures from other bulls.

The exception was Oliver's brassy solo skim to challenge Nick and Rick (Picture 77). One, junior bull Oliver performed his barreling bull display alone, illustrating his daring. Two, it drew the senior bulls into a sprinting pursuit and cornering the culprit although they did not actually fight.

PICTURE 80

*Bonded bulls use **unison skims** to great effect when they barrel past a dolphin group or slam through the middle of it, scattering individuals. This behavior's speed and splashes give it center stage. It is a swift display that erupts in tense situations involving several bulls as a demonstration of the performing pair's unified power and pugnacity.*

Leap: Unison Leap to Escape Aggressive Bulls

PICTURE 81

A mother dolphin may leap to gain speed and draw her calf alongside to elude harassment from bulls on the rare occasions that escape is necessary. Here, Bette curls around and pulls her baby Ballou along in an envelope of water to escape marauding males Mike and Lax. Because bottlenose dolphins are the world's best imitators after people, calves soon learn to leap when mom does.

It is uncommon for bulls to be hostile towards calves on the "Enchanted River." We have only seen ten cases in 14,000 encounters. In most of those, one or more dolphins came to the rescue of the harassed dolphins. Therefore, mothers and calves leaping to escape hostile bulls is a rare sight too.

Only three times in 15 years have we seen two bulls harass a calf at length. In one of these exceptional episodes, Gazio and W.R. sprinted all the way across a bay to antagonize a mother and her young calf by trapping them under a dock. The bad bulls' long distance sprint says, to me, that they had clear intent to provoke aggression.

Leap: Unison Leap to Avoid Pesky Teens

PICTURE 82

Mother-calf pairs may use the unison skim to avoid pesky teens. In this picture, the social setting involves a mother-calf pair and male teens who commandeer the calf and march it helplessly around the seas. When other dolphins arrive and intervene, the mother and son leap free of the water, as shown here, and escape at speed.

***

On the "Enchanted River" leaps signify serious business. I do not believe dolphins leap in play. In contrast, the aerial behaviors in the next chapter have a range of uses from play and popular tools of teasing to serious social business.

CHAPTER 7

Why Dolphins Slap

PICTURE 83

*A **slap** occurs when a dolphin strikes some part of its body against the water surface, another dolphin, or some other surface. The dolphin in this picture is slapping the left side of its head against the water, called a **side head slap**. Dolphins who have been injured may do side head slaps against the water surface, as in this picture, like a human pounding a headache against a pillow.*

Like breaches, slaps are named for the body part that is slapped: chin slaps, side head slaps, back head slaps, pectoral fin slaps, and tail slaps. When a dolphin slaps more than half of its body, it is usually called a breach. Dolphins slap the way humans slap: on a range from playful or symbolic through serious to striking as hard as one can. Dolphins use slaps for a stunning number of reasons.

The most common slaps among the dolphins of the "Enchanted River" are tail slaps, in which a dolphin strikes its flukes or entire tailstock. Tail slaps range in form from subtle to conspicuous. The subtlest are mere flicks of the flukes. The most conspicuous are forceful whacks that shovel or even aerosolize the water into fine droplets.

PICTURE 84
*The **superb** control of a dolphin slapping its tail is hard to fathom but worth keeping in mind when reading this chapter. Two vivid demonstrations of its purposeful power might suffice.*

Tail Slap: Personal Wet T-shirt Contest

One vivid demonstration of the purposeful power and superb control of a tailslapping dolphin resulted in my starring role in a very personal wet T-shirt contest, compliments of a captive dolphin in an enclosed Florida lagoon. A fresh college graduate ostensibly searching for my destiny, I was at the moment jammed shoulder-to-shoulder between other tourists along the railing of a dolphin tour boat, ostensibly searching for dolphins in an enclosed lagoon.

PICTURE 85
A dolphin living in the lagoon surfaced near the dolphin tour boat and sur-
veyed the familiar wall of anonymous grins lining the boat's railing. It made
its decision, cocked its tail, swiped it across the surface, and slammed a
wall of water against our side of the boat.

I was soaked! This soaking is burned into my memory for two reasons. First, I was the only person who was soaked. Impossibly, the two people I was jammed between were dry, which with pointing fingers they found hilarious. Second, it was hip at the time to go bra-less. My dilemma was suddenly that of a young, lone woman traveler wearing a clingy, see-through T-shirt but no bra. (No picture available)

At the time I thought the captive dolphin's aim was astonishing. My guess is that it had been perfecting its marvelous technique for a long time, especially once it learned that the gesture guaranteed a yelping reaction from the grinning guests jammed shoulder to shoulder along the railing of the dolphin tour boat.

Tail Slap: When Startled

Another vivid demonstration of the purposeful power and superb control of a tailslapping dolphin involved the wild dolphin who taught me that a dolphin may slap its tail when startled.

Just before dawn one cool spring night, I dozed in my bed and listened to sea sounds through open windows. A great blue heron announced its location with rasping cries. Its shy cousin, a night heron, gave a squeakier call that hid its location.

From the water came a small tinkling sound, the belly flop of a mullet. These tasty fish periodically chuck themselves out of the water and drop back in with small tinkling belly flops. They leap to draw a deep breath but inadvertently announce their location to predators too, their splash landing sites becoming targets of glassy, slowly-expanding circles.

The next tinkling belly flop was followed by a bassoon of a sound as a large creature slammed a wall of water against the seawall. Mullet are prey to many large predators. Predators

PICTURE 86

What also struck me was that the dolphin knew that I was there at all. Dolphin eyes are low on the sides of their head and usually underwater when they surface to breathe. Why was it looking above the surface in the dark? It submerged and resumed its search for breakfast without answering.

with enough bulk to slam walls of water like that as they spin to catch a frantic fish include bottlenose dolphins and bull sharks. Whose ever spinning bulk had slammed water against that seawall, the thought of being alone with it in those dark waters made me shudder and catch my breath. Reveling in the safety of my bed, I exhaled slowly.

The next sound was an exhalation too, but not mine. The hunter was a dolphin. As it lunged after another fish, I lunged too - out of bed and down to the end of our dock where I sat cross-legged and silent at water's edge. In the hush of pre-dawn, I tracked the dolphin's location by the intermittent sounds of its breaths. Why is it easier to hear in the dark of night than in the light of day? The dolphin surfaced far to my right. Though disappointed that it hunted in the distance, I marveled to be listening to a wild dolphin at all and one I might even recognize. It was like meditating.

Suddenly the dolphin surfaced off our dock inches from me - so close that I instinctively flinched.

My flinch startled the dolphin. Its powerful tail rose over the water, hung for an ominous moment, and then simply popped back down into a fitful little tail slap. Tiny drops of water spritzed my face.

"Sorry to startle you!" I cried into the dark.

Postscript. I stayed until dawn to see if the dolphin stayed and if I knew who it was. It was Nick, a principal member of the Bowery Boys super-alliance of bulls. He was startled by my unexpected presence because dolphins can become engrossed, especially when hunting and socializing. Engrossed dolphins are inattentive to their surroundings, similar to the way people on their cell phones are inattentive. Thus, boaters and Jet Ski enthusiasts need to watch out for dolphins and manatees, not the other way around. Nick could have tailslapped the water hard enough to drench me but chose not to.

***

Dolphins along the "Enchanted River" seem to use tail slaps the most often among themselves to attract attention for two opposite communiqués: warnings to go away or invitations to approach. As such, tail slaps are a good example of how dolphins use the same behavior for different reasons. To discern meaning, such as play versus irritation, observers must watch for clues. It might help to visualize the many ways a person uses a slap. How is the slap thrown? Is the tailstock loose or rigid? Does the slap hit something? If so, how hard? What happens next?

Warning Tail Slaps

Tail Slap: Warning Away a Shark

The Seminole Indians of old Florida were well-acquainted with the habits of local sharks. Regrettably, that knowledge has been lost. Today, the sharks' habits are mysterious. I wish we could ask the dolphins what they know about sharks.

One autumn day, two members of the Bowery Boys super-alliance of bulls, Nick and Rick, shot past with two local ladies. The quartet rushed a quarter mile to a rendezvous with two other big bulls, Simon and Xavier. Long acquaintances, the quartet and pair fell into step easily. As two trios of a lady and two bulls each, they leisurely covered the next quarter mile together as if they were waltzing. Such relaxed dolphins can hypnotize observers.

Shattering their indolent rhythm, Xavier brusquely raised his tail as high as he could and slammed it down on the water surface as hard as he could. He quickly gave a second resounding tailslap, again with full force. "Take that!" his slaps seemed to say. But why? To whom?

PICTURE 87
The dolphins swam right past the shark basking under the surface! Evidently, six passing dolphins – sleepy or not - did not have to veer away from one shark. This time.

When Xavier tail slapped, we had been paralleling the drowsy dolphins in the boat some twenty feet away. In the event that he had slugged the water to warn us to back off, Capt. John clicked the throttle into neutral gear so the dolphins could increase the distance between us if they chose. At that moment, our fish-finding sonar glared with the giant icon of a shark behind our boat. We had just glided over it.

Would Xavier's resounding tail slaps have worked to warn the shark away if he had been alone without his five schoolmates? Do sharks remember such episodes or the dolphins involved? As I watched the sleepy sextet cover the next quarter mile as if waltzing, I again wished we could ask dolphins what they know about sharks.

***

Tail slaps play a big role in the contests of courtship. Pregnant females occasionally warn away approaching bulls by slapping their tails or chest on the water. More often, it is females who are theoretically available for dating and mating (technically available females) who slap to warn away unsuitable suitors.

Tail Slap: Female Warning Away a Male

Female dolphins on the "Enchanted River" choose whether to accept or reject male company. Rejecting unwanted male attention does not require a female to leap into the air or even leave the vicinity altogether. A well-placed tail slap will do.

PICTURE 88

One autumn day, five months after her tailstock was brutally sliced by the indifferent blades of a passing boat propeller, Babyface swims with a dozen other dolphins. Several suitors bid for her attention by coming up and nudging her from behind. She rejects each in turn by slapping him in the face with her flukes! The slaps were reassuring evidence that her tailstock still worked despite its disfigurement.

***

The showiest tail slaps in the courtship arena are performed by two dolphins at the same time, called synchronized or unison tail slaps, or in coordinated alternation, called syncopated tail slaps. Both versions reveal that the two tailslapping dolphins are cooperating with each other. Both versions indicate a partnership, whether long-term or temporary, and communicate the shared state of mind of a united front. Just as people recognize what another person is trying to accomplish and sometimes help by coordinating with them, sometimes in their own interests, dolphins do too. Coordinated slaps are uncommon. They are hard to film because they occur without warning and are rarely repeated.

Tail Slap: Bonded Bulls Warning Away a Rival

One might expect bonded bull buddies who are courting females to synchronize their slaps as double warnings to rival bulls, and they do. The shallow waters around the islands of The Pass are popular dolphin gathering grounds. Such "sandbar socials" typically include technically available females, bulls who compete for them, and females with calves of various ages. Teens are notably absent, though occasionally spotted on the far edges of the action as they tune in to the adults' interactions as if to a radio broadcast of a baseball game.

One June evening, 18 dolphins gathered, mostly bulls amid a handful of pregnant and mother dolphins, and Sybil - the only female of interest to the bulls. Her newborn calf had died three weeks before, propelling her into a technically available phase that drew bulls like ants to crumbs. Side by side, the females threaded through swirling suitors busy sizing each other up – like a lively human bar scene. A lone bull approached the ladies but was chased away by a bull pair, in turn chased away by another bull pair, Orson and Welles.

PICTURE 89
Out-gunned by the synchronized pair of bulls, big burly bull Nick vanishes.
He would, however, be back.

A member of the Bowery Boys super-alliance and temporarily without his own alliance partner, Nick was one of the lone bulls. Nick knew Sybil well and had shown a strong interest in her (some bulls of the "Enchanted River" show a steady preference for the same female across the years). When Nick arrived on this evening's social scene, he headed straight for her.

At the time, the females were flanked by big bulls Orson and Welles. Their response to Nick's arrival was to wind up and whack their beefy tails against the water at the same time in a conspicuous synchronized tail slap. This startled the youngest calf in the group, Celine, so her mother scooped her up on her back for a short and slippery but reassuring ride.

Tail Slap: Courting Couples Warning Away Rivals

Courting couples occasionally coordinate their tail slaps too, warning away rivals together! More surprising for warnings, some tail slaps are subtle – almost symbolic. For example, when big bull Simon is courting a female, he has the habit of performing one or more series of light taps of the flukes against the water when romantic rivals draw too near, behavior called motorboating. Females echo his warnings by doing the same!

One amorous June morning in 2014, for example, courting couple Simon and Bette was trailed by two rival bulls. When the rivals swirled too closely, Simon started a series of subtle tail slaps – subtle like an ominous drumbeat – which Bette quickly matched. One amorous July morning five years later in 2019, courting couple Simon and Sybil was trailed by four rival bulls. Again when rivals swirled too closely, Simon performed his series of subtle tail slaps – which Sybil then matched.

In both episodes, rivals dropped back. Though biologically compelled to continue tracking a fertile female, rival bulls ceased to challenge the reigning escort Simon - for the moment. How can Simon afford to use subtle tail slaps? He has high status and therefore no need to fight to have his way.

Such observations show that bottlenose dolphins of the "Enchanted River" watch each other and match or imitate each other in social situations that call for communicating a united front. They reveal that a pair of bulls does not automatically prevail against a lone bull when male rivals compete for a fertile female. They also show that courting couples may act in unison, similar to the way bonded bulls act in unison, to communicate a united front.

Tail Slap: Female Friends Keep Suitors at Bay

Female friends may also synchronize tail slaps, working together to warn away suitors. One calm winter day, the seas were anything but calm as two female and four bull dolphins sprinted around wildly as small wads.

The sextet tumbled over one another in rolling invitations, mount attempts, slapping "belly flop" reprisals, wiggling departures, and rapid returns for more – every move done with exaggeration and the suddenness of exploding fireworks. Bulls behave like this in the presence of attractive females as much to draw their attention by stylin' with exaggerated moves, as to remind the other bulls of their competitive edge. This is high energy at sea!

Waylaid from every side, females PeeWee and Trix charged side by side through the spirited throng as females often do when surrounded by swirling, stylin' bulls. Whenever I see

PICTURE 90
Trix does a chin slap as Scrapefin Sam mounts her and keeps a sharp look-out out for rivals.

PICTURE 91
Maturing females may use syncopated tail slaps to keep suitors at bay. This picture shows the smashing tail end of a syncopated display of tail slaps by teen females PeeWee and Trix in the face of would-be suitor Ski. Alas, their coordinated gesture failed to deter him. At least they had each other.

females glued together in this sexy context, I get the impression that they coordinate closely to obtain social leverage that neither female would have without the other.

At one point, Ski drew too close and triggered the girls' syncopated tail slaps. I do not know if he actually poked PeeWee, but Ski was following them closely when PeeWee suddenly swung up into a headstand and on the down-stroke whacked water into Ski's face. As PeeWee ended her tail slap, Trix started hers, swinging up into a headstand and on her down-stroke also whacking water into Ski's face.

Tail Slap: The Most Aggressive

PICTURE 92

*A **tail whip** is the most aggressive of the tail slaps. In the tail whip shown here, an angry dolphin strikes by cocking its tailstock back and releasing it like a coiled spring with the power to break a person's neck. This is no longer a warning. It is a direct assault.*

PICTURE 93

A tail whip characterizes the most serious of confrontations. Persons in kayaks or on paddleboards who see one or two dolphins "doing cartwheels" are most earnestly advised to keep their distance. Never approach. The animals are locked in desperate combat and see only the fighting. People drawing near innocently could be injured accidentally.

PICTURE 94

We witnessed a serious bull fight over Independence Day in 2013 in the shallows of The Pass, just off sandbars crowded with lovers and families for the holiday. Fighting dolphins create lots of splashes. Attracted to the hubbub, people lined the edges of the water and enjoyed the dolphins the way they would the spectacle of a passing parade, pointing and ooh-ing and ahh-ing.

PICTURE 95

The problem was that the crowd on the sandbar did not realize that the dolphins were fighting in earnest. This became obvious when a dad prepared to launch his young son and daughter into kayaks to go out and see the dolphins close up, like sending one's 5-year-old into a mosh pit. Capt. John and I gestured wildly and shouted warnings to stay away from the fighting dolphins.

I have never received so many dirty looks in my life.

**

Invitational Tail Slaps

Dolphins along the "Enchanted River" also use tail slaps as invitations to approach. Early in these pages, I told three stories about two dolphins and one elephant who started dancing around and attracted our attention. Dolphins also "start dancing around" to attract attention from other dolphins. Extreme efforts involve aerial behaviors, like Yukon's jumping in his mom's face to get her to play (Picture 20) and Sylvia's amorous athleticism for Puck (Picture 22).

Lesser attention-getting behaviors – which on land we call teasing and flirting - involve an arsenal of changes in body position loosely performed by playful and relaxed dolphins (read: wiggly). Flirty dolphins attract attention by rolling in the water in full or partial corkscrews, sometimes with a coquettish flip of a fluke peaking out of the water surface; by bopping up and down vertically like a kid bouncing on a pogo stick (behavior called spyhopping), and slapping various body parts.

Tail Slap: A Female Teasing a Bull

Dolphins may tail slap to tease another dolphin. While writing this book, Capt. John and I had a captivating episode whose finale included the teasing tail slap shown in Picture 96.

PICTURE 96
*Wound-up by the end of their surfing saga, the three dolphins began to flirt. Trix led the bulls through a floating matte of seagrass. After adorning herself with kelly-green blades of turtle grass (attention-getting behavior called **self decoration**), she wafts into a headstand and thwacks the water lightly as shown here. Following close behind her, this earned Juno a face full of sparkling water.*

One June morning with clouds crowding overhead, we spotted two dolphins in the distance and headed over across a shallow bay. To our delight, they sped directly over to us too. They were two junior bulls whom we had not seen in two years, Juno and Scarface. They asked to surf our boat by hugging it so closely and persistently that we finally sped up. The two bulls surfed our boat waves for the next half hour, the longest episode of surfing dolphins I have ever seen.

Spontaneous souls if there ever were any, at some point a third dolphin dropped what she was doing and joined them, Trix. They surfed and leapt and spun and crisscrossed our wake for five exhilarating miles.

The trio socialized easily for several more minutes, and then went their separate ways as abruptly as they had joined together.

Tail Slap: Teasing the Researcher

One spring day, we found mother-calf pair Celeste and Celine. Deep in the driving hunger of late pregnancy, Celeste was focused on feeding. Celine, now 5 years old, zipped around in search of action like baby monkeys when their monkey folks are napping. Intent on energizing the situation however she could, Celine came over to our stodgy old research boat and smacked her tail repeatedly to persuade us to speed up so she could surf our waves. I braced against the boat railing and leaned out as far over the water as I could, aiming my camera at this sea sprite I had so affectionately watched grow up.

PICTURE 97
*Teasing dolphins may start a tail slap but not finish it. In this picture, Celine threatens to soak me by slapping the water with her tail but instead slid back into the water without a splash. Incomplete expressions of a behavior, like Celine's unfinished tail slap, are called **intention behaviors** - someone intends to do something, but stops after an initial gesture without completing it. It is possible that Celine did her **intention tail slap** instead of a full tail slap to avoid getting me wet.*

She surfaced in front of me and lifted her tailstock in preparation for another tailslap. This put my camera in grave danger of a fatal salt water shower. Celine wound up her tailstock as shown in Picture 97 and swung it down with force. Just short of smacking the water, however, she stopped and merely slid into the sea with nary a splash!

Besides teasing, intention tail slaps have other uses. New mother dolphins do intention tail slaps to threaten a boat that has followed her and the new baby for too long or too closely. The mere threat to slap may serve a double purpose: warning the boater without scaring the newborn by whacking the water next to it.

Dolphins can tap their tails as lightly as a feather settling on the ground, as when mom dolphins pet their calves with an affectionate sweep of the flukes. Calves may tap big bulls to invite them to play. A dolphin may tap our boat in greeting, like the time big bull Nick veered over as he raced past and tapped our boat before speeding on. For a small number of specialists, however, tail slaps can even be used to find something to eat.

***

Feeding Tail Slaps

Tail Slap: Whacking at a Seaside Wimbledon

Another tail slap that brilliantly showcases a dolphin's physical power and control is a super-sized version used to disorient fish or pop them senseless: a kerplunk.

Kerplunking is an expert technique. Its power and control makes it the maritime counterpart to professional tennis. It is only used by a handful of dolphin specialists who hit fish instead of tennis balls, but chase them just as fervently.

PICTURE 98
With a single focused strike of her tailstock called a kerplunk, Sylvia sends a fountain of water into the air as high as our 20-foot research boat is long.

PICTURE 99

A kerplunk is a specialized feeding tail slap that creates two shock waves, shown in this picture. The first shoots a small shear of water backwards. The second shoots a fountain of water vertically many more feet into the air. The double shock on the water accounts for this behavior's strange name, an onomatopoeia for the two-pronged sound made by slapping the tailstock just so: ker-PLUNK!

Like tennis, kerplunks take practice. Mother dolphins sometimes appear to actively demonstrate the technique while their calves appear to copy them for practice. What characterizes these apparent practice sessions is that the dolphins alternate kerplunks. First, the mother does a few kerplunks. Then, her calf does a few kerplunks, back and forth, over and over.

One of these potential practice sessions occurred one December in a hidden cove in our study area. Sylvia and her two-year-old calf Saltan alternated kerplunks for over half an hour. Sylvia's kerplunks were direct and controlled. Saltan's kerplunks were tentative, wobbly, and often incomplete: The youngster would elevate its tail gingerly but, as if it found this unusual position too awkward, often slid back into the sea without slapping it. Mother and calf performed enough kerplunks in a small spot of water that day to provide me with a first-rate collection of photos and videos with which to study this specialized technique.

***

Uses of Other Types of Slaps

Tailslaps are the most frequent of the slaps, but there are other types too. Back slaps, chin slaps, and side slaps seem to range from relaxed vivaciousness to quarrelsome or fiery. They are often difficult to interpret. Because dolphins will flee from events that disturb them, it is hard to determine the tone of the exchange when they remain in episodes that look rough to human observers.

PICTURE 100

A **back slap** occurs when a dolphin pops its head and chest out of the water and drops backwards. Here, Scrapefin Sam drops into a friendly back slap during light jousting with Vic, the latter potentially taking his first steps up the bottlenose bull social ladder.

PICTURE 101

A **chin slap** occurs when a dolphin pops its head and chest out of the water and drops forward. Here, Trix rises so high to slap her chest, it is hard to say if this is an extreme chin slap or restrained belly breach. The youngest of a spirited group of teens on this winter day, Trix matches her slap-happy schoolmates by slapping repeatedly. Note how she clenches her teeth.

PICTURE 102

A female may use a smooth back slap to lie back in the water to communicate disinterest. Here, Sylvia whooshes effortlessly into a back slap to ward off schoolmates. Just before this picture, bonded bulls Nick and Rick had flanked her and performed a synchronized tail slap. If that meant to persuade her, it did not work, for she proceeded to do back slaps, as in this picture, until all the bulls left her alone except Puck, the bull for whom she eventually performed her amorous athleticism (shown in Pictures 22 & 136).

PICTURE 103

*Vic whooshes backward into a more vigorous back slap called a **lay back** to avoid a lunging schoolmate by slapping him with water. This is during an increasingly testy episode in Vic's early ascent up the bull social ladder, during which he was baited by bigger bulls.*

PICTURE 104

A stronger slap in closer proximity, still without contact, makes a stronger point.

PICTURE 105

*As tensions rise, one dolphin may back slap another dolphin by falling on it deliberately, so the gesture is called a fall-on. The **fall-on** gesture occurs across a range from affectionate to aggressive, more frequently aggressive.*

PICTURE 106

In highly aggressive settings, a dolphin slaps hard on a rival who presses up from underneath in a concerted counterattack. Fall-ons are typical during conflicts. Although the elasticity of the water cushions the blow, imagine being body-slammed by 500 pounds.

Retaliatory Side Slap: Calf Warns Mother

PICTURE 107

Calves can become annoyed with their mothers and threaten to slap her. Here, young Prism launches up and threatens to fall on his mother, Queen Priscilla, retaliating against her discipline. Ultimately, however, he simply showered her with a cascade of daunting waves. Mother-calf disputes are settled quickly.

Back Tail Slap: Inverted Motorboating

PICTURE 108

*A dolphin may perform a series of tail slaps while swimming on its back, behavior called **inverted motorboating**. I have seen females perform this behavior whose mammaries were swollen with milk or whose genital fields were raw with irritation. I have seen a bull perform a couple sets of inverted motorboating in the context of several bulls competing for a female by stylin' with various exaggerated behaviors.*

Back Slap: Reveals Unsuspected Condition

PICTURE 109

Like other aerial behaviors, slaps may reveal information otherwise hidden by the sea. Here, Scarface's back slap reveals that discarded fishing line has become wrapped around his left pectoral fin. The bit of yellow is a remnant of artificial bait. The small round bulge at the top of his fin is a hunk of skin where the fishing line slowly saws his fin off.

PICTURE 110

Four months later, a chance back head slap reveals that the fishing line wrapped around Scarface's left pectoral fin is gone. How it was removed remains a mystery. The scar remains where it sliced deep into his fin.

***

Slaps may or may not embellish the aerial behaviors featured in the next chapter.

CHAPTER 8

Why Dolphins Spyhop

PICTURE 111

*A **spyhop** is the dolphin version of rearing up. A spyhop occurs when a dolphin bounces or springs out of the water in a vertical or near-vertical position. Here, Celine's spyhop creates a surreal gray dolphin against winter green seas. In practice, the amount of body exposed above the surface typically varies from just the head to past the belly button, although more of the body is exposed on rare occasions. A charming but rare variation is a spyhopping dolphin who spins like a corkscrew.*

Spyhop: Seeing South of the Belly Button

Spyhops are pretty and useful. Early in our study, moms Sybil and Xanadu allowed their yearling calves to cavort at our boat. Playing baby dolphins are quicksilver. They zing through liquid space, making fools of photographers. As long as one's heart is not set on a prize photo, this feature makes them irresistible.

Learning each dolphin's gender and to tell dolphins apart on sight, recognizing each as a unique individual, are two monumental challenges of a study of dolphin behavior at sea. The typical dolphin withholds clues as to whether it is male or female. The exception is the adult dolphin who is consistently seen with a calf and who is therefore assumed to be a female because it is assumed to be the calf's mother. However, because most mammals show sex-related differences in behavior, such as cooperative lionesses compared to murderous male lions, it is essential to know if a dolphin is a male or a female to understand dolphin behavior. After naming Steve with ease, I remained blissfully unaware that identifying the gender of the next 300 dolphins would take years!

***

Spyhops from the Start

Calves like Steve are keen on spyhops. They spyhop from the start of life. Two reasons are their initial lack of physical coordination and their pitching forward from the momentum of mom's swimming. It also seems to me that another part is the innocent joi de vivre of all baby mammals.

PICTURE 112
Without warning, a calf pops up out of the water like a kid on a pogo stick, revealing that he was a male. I promptly named him Steve to alphabetize with his mom Sybil. The photo of his bright-eyed spyhop was one of sporadic photographic successes early in my career as a dolphin behaviorist and remains a prized possession.

Spyhop: Darting Breath

PICTURE 113

*Newborn bottlenose dolphins take at least three months to learn to swim with the smooth rhythm of the adults. Before that, they seem to stumble up out of the water in a winsome behavior called a **darting breath**. Here, Courtney's newborn demonstrates the darting breath while mom keeps an eye on her baby with a backward glance. Newborn status is indicated by the dark color and stripes called fetal folds, wrinkles left over from the close confines of the uterus.*

Spyhop: Water Play

PICTURE 114

As a baby dolphin develops its aquatic bearings, its spyhops become more deliberate than accidental. Some babies discover that spyhops are handy for water play, as Xanadu's son shows here.

Spyhop: Energy to Burn

PICTURE 115

Dolphin calves are wiggly creatures with energy to burn, often prancing at their mother's side. Here, next to his mom Faye, 3-month-old Falco prances across the cooling waters of his first autumn at sea. The energy of his lunges and splashes upon his re-entry may keep his mother Faye informed about how lively or sleepy he feels.

Spyhop: Reaction to Getting Goosed

As the calf ages, its spyhops shift from clumsy swimming to social gestures.

PICTURE 116

Four-month-old Celine does a surprised spyhop after being goosed by a playmate. This was one of the first times that her watchful mother Celeste allowed young Celine to play with schoolmates, and their unfamiliar nudges startled her into spyhops. This is her first set of toothrakes, too.

Spyhop: Belly Display

PICTURE 117
Saga spyhops in the eye of a playmate. His gesture seems perfectly placed to put his belly button and regions south of it on display. This behavior suggests that dolphins may use spyhops as genital displays, and if so, do so from a young age.

Spyhop: A Stimulating Winter Romp

PICTURE 118
The bottlenose dolphins of the "Enchanted River" frolic the most frequently when the water is cool, mid 60s to low 70s °F. Here, young Cardio (named for his high activity level) lurches out of the cool waters of February in a **bent-head spyhop**, *wound up from the excitement of a good-natured wrestling match and surfing with Cody, three years older than he. His white lines and dots are slashes and pocks, respectively, from youthful contact with sharp oyster shells and perhaps urchin spines. White is part of the healing process.*

Spyhop: Excited Reaction to a Strange New Playmate

Spyhopping dolphins are excited, often pleasantly so. One early spring day, adult dolphins searched a small bay for breakfast while their youngest member, Delta, searched for amusement. A young cormorant, tan and tawny with a long neck and narrow hooked beak, landed nearby. Floating, it submerged its head, as if having a look around underwater, and created the bizarre image of a headless bird.

Young Delta swam to the headless bird and floated in front of it with his head cocked underwater as if he was having a look around too. In actuality, duck and dolphin were having a good look at each other; then both dove, surfaced, and did it again! It was the drollest interspecific episode I have ever seen. It was on the heels of this natural introduction that Delta started spyhopping.

PICTURE 119
Young Delta spyhops in the exciting aftermath of meeting a strange new playmate. I was unable to obtain photos of both the baby dolphin and cormorant because only one or the other was visible at the surface at any given time, the more-mobile baby dolphin typically swirling just under the water surface in front of the bird.

Spyhop: Snapping at Shadows

One autumn afternoon, a dolphin calf amused herself as she waited for her mother to finish hunting. She dashed here and there, visited passing boats, and even tried to surf the least promising wavelets. She wiggled over and followed us around in the starboard wingman position, jiggling as only a young dolphin can.

PICTURE 120

Something caught the young dolphin's attention. She popped out of the water in a small spyhop and cocked her head sideways like a bird to get a better look at it. To get an even better look, she slipped underwater and rolled upside down, aiming both her eyes at the object that had caught her attention. We could not see what she was looking at.

When the time came to move on, Capt. John pulled away very slowly. The little lady followed us in her wingman position, periodically spyhopping and snapping at the object that had caught her attention. The scene reminded me of slowly leading a horse by dangling a carrot. We still could not see what she was looking at.

When I suddenly saw the little dolphin's "carrot," I laughed. She was snapping at the shadow of our boat's flag on the water surface!

Spyhop: Feeling Good Again

Researchers can tell a certain amount about the condition of a wild dolphin by what it does but also by what it does not do, behavior I refer to as *in absentia*. For example, sick and injured dolphins do not play or only dabble at it dispiritedly. Once a calf begins to play normally again, it seems reasonable to say that it feels better.

Young Juno became wrapped in discarded fishing line in the fall of 2008 as a 6-month-old and did not play during this time. By January, the fishing line was mysteriously gone. Juno scampered around that bright winter day in extraordinary good spirits. He spyhopped so many times in his mother Jay's hunting patch that she finally came over and poked him to calm him down. It took two more pokes before he understood her message and finally calmed down.

***

PICTURE 121
*Juno's **bent-head spyhop** reveals a curious skin condition characterized by rust-colored patches on his lower jaw that was only exposed by his spyhops.*

Spyhop: Spyhopping Whales

Whales spyhop, too. Whales that stop to spyhop along shorelines, like the gray whale in Picture 122, provide a precious prehistoric image in these modern times of cash and condos and cars. It is said that migrating whales spyhop to search the shoreline silhouette for map markers to see where they are.

As this interpretation of spyhopping whales suggests, spyhops are likely to function at least in part to give a marine mammal a glimpse of the world above the water. However, they function in other ways as well. A baby gray whale once came over to our San Diego research boat. Charmed, we were leaning over the side of the boat for a better look when its massive mother reared out of the water between her baby and our boat, her wide eye above us glaring down with hot suspicion. Daunted, we fell back as the sudden silhouette of her spyhop blocked out the sun.

***

Good Spirits

Along the "Enchanted River," spyhops can occur any time of year. Yet they are three times as likely to occur from late fall through early spring than across

PICTURE 122
For years I watched gray whales spyhop along the San Diego shores on their migrations north to gorge in Alaska or south to mate and give birth in Baja. I wondered how they kept their maps up to date as humanity changed shoreline silhouettes with a never-ending stream of new buildings.

PICTURE 123

A spyhopping dolphin appears dry. Oliver's spyhop illustrates how easily dolphin skin sheds water, lacking the friction of human skin against water. Dolphin skin sheds so rapidly that the outer layers are replaced every two hours.

the heat of summer. Therefore, they may be cool water behaviors, broadly parallel to an athletic person who jogs or cycles during cool mornings rather than hot afternoons.

Unlike the glaring mother gray whale, it also seems to me that spyhops are usually "fair weather" behaviors along the "Enchanted River." That is, spyhops occasionally occur during contention, most notably as the graceful double spyhop as in Picture 5. Otherwise, spyhopping dolphins tend to be unperturbed rather than edgy.

Spyhopping dolphins also tend to be teens. Teen dolphins are the most active dolphins, frequently seen socializing at sea in riotous groups. Physically rowdy and socially agile, teens are good for many demonstrations of the roles of aerial behaviors. Spyhops often take center stage in their exchanges because teens are highly social, like our own teens on land, and by this age spyhops tend to be social gestures.

Spyhops are easy to recognize but vary in form when they melt into other behaviors that together create a more complex move made up of several behaviors though performed fluidly. For example, the standard spyhopping dolphin ends its maneuver by sliding back down into the water the way it slid up out of it. Variations include a spyhopping dolphin who curls forward and somersaults its way back in or who slaps its way back in. As the next several pictures show, there are many variations from which to choose.

Spyhop: Pure Play

PICTURE 124

As a young teen, Oliver twists his way back into the water during a boister-ous afternoon during which several teens and calves gave countless fluid demonstrations of aerial behavior (except leaping).

PICTURE 125

Another fluid demonstration involved two teens in a double spyhop, lurch-ing up together in a closely coordinated move. Play is a good time to prac-tice coordinating, and coordination is a revealing part of bottlenose dolphin social behavior.

PICTURE 126

Two dolphins who spyhop in tandem may push each other. This pretty shoulder-shoving maneuver can be used in play or conflict. It is play in this picture.

PICTURE 127

*Spyhops easily melt into **fall-on** behaviors, too, in which a dolphin rears up and drops down on a schoolmate. This picture shows a lighthearted fall-on complete with a playface, though landings range from gentle to hard.*

PICTURE 128
A teen dolphin in especially good spirits may draw on water play from its youth, as Babyface illustrates here.

Spyhop: Bouncing Around the Political Arena

Play fades as a dolphin grows up and serious social matters take priority. A maturing male dolphin has a tall social ladder to climb because he must establish himself in the hierarchy of other males. Like chimps, young male dolphins initially learn about bull behavior from watching his

PICTURE 129
Vidalia performs a high spyhop while flanked by senior bulls Nick and Rick (submerged and not visible), potentially displaying his belly to them. The long slit off the corner of his mouth under his eye is a scar from discarded fishing line that became wedged like a bridle and slit the corners of his mouth.

mother's bull companions. What he learns depends on how they behave, such as remaining composed or becoming quarrelsome. His ascent up the social ladder may begin when he is still a calf with his mother (before weaning), perhaps in forging early friendships that reap future political good will.

Four years old in Picture 129, Vidalia's interactions with the senior bulls had lost the breathless excitement and ambivalence of dashing calves. He and Nick even made a brief statement of unity by swimming side-by-side in synchrony for a moment. This episode marked a new social phase for young Vidalia.

Nick and Rick had accompanied Vidalia and his mother Valiant several times in the previous weeks before Picture 129 was taken, suggesting that they were warming up to court her. Yet, noting the easy interaction between all three males during this time, and similar settings with other males, I wonder if bottlenose dolphins show a political parallel to baboons. In her fascinating book, "Sex and Friendship in Baboons," primatologist Barbara Smuts showed that male baboons invest tremendous attention and affection in a baby baboon whose mother they wish to mate. Might bottlenose bulls like Nick and Rick, who are interested in a mother dolphin like Valiant, curry favor from her offspring like Vidalia? It is an intriguing possibility.

On the other hand, bottlenose bulls build complex social networks among themselves based on long-term bonds. Bulls like Nick may be just as interested in having a relationship with a mother's son as with his mother - maybe even more interested. After all, fertile females come and go. One's political relationships with other bulls must be maintained, potentially for decades.

PICTURE 130
*Scrapefin Sam and Vic demonstrate the role of **shoulder-shoving spyhops** during Vic's early introduction to the bottlenose bullpen. Years later, as of this writing, the two bulls remain more likely to cooperate than compete. The tone of these early exchanges may set the stage for future relations.*

***

Sizzling Seas
Spyhop: Sex Face

PICTURE 131

*The dolphins of the "Enchanted River" may pause during sex to spyhop as shown here. The sexual context and gleaming expression earned this minimal spyhop-with-glance combination the moniker of **sex face**, a behavior that only occurs during sexual encounters. The expression makes one wonder what is going on underwater.*

Spyhop: Display Pink Chests

Before I knew that bottlenose dolphins' bright white bellies can flush a range of shades from pastel to deep pink, I named a deep-pink-bellied dolphin "Pepto" after the deep pink stomach-soothing medicine Pepto Bismal™. Years later, when Pepto bonded with a bull buddy, we naturally called the latter "Bismal."

It is uncommon to see a spyhopping dolphin with a pink belly. It is more common to see a rolling dolphin with a white belly, the flicker of white said to serve as an eye-catching social signal in the gloom of the undersea world. The bouncing belly of a spyhopping dolphin ought to be eye-catching for the same reason. When a spyhop occurs around other dolphins, it is tempting to see it as a social behavior used to display one's self.

PICTURE 132

A dolphin who spyhops high enough may reveal its pink chest, which flushes in a variety of circumstances. Some type of aerial behavior is necessary to reveal pink chests to boat-based observers.

Spyhop: Good Spirits from Agreeable Company

PICTURE 133

Cody bounces out of the water in a spyhop and eyes the water for schoolmates trying to poke her again. The point of this teen exercise seemed to be Cody as the target, her belly as the bull's eye, and her three schoolmates as the arrows. Between spyhops, Cody rafts on her side on the water surface, holding her pectoral fin up in the air like a waving arm. One or two schoolmates come over and bump her belly. This makes her curl and roll over, sometimes flipping her flukes in their faces.

PICTURE 134

Trix uses a spyhop to bob in front of Scrapefin Sam and Ski as they approach her in unison. Her striking white belly contrasts with the two bulls' dark backs. This darker-above-lighter-below color scheme, called countershading, is a form of camouflage that makes a dolphin harder to see in the sun-drenched waters of the photic zone.

PICTURE 135

As his bonded bull buddy Nick watches from the sidelines, Rick spyhops repeatedly during his courtship with Bette. Here, Rick leans back into the water from a spyhop as he mouths a fish lightheartedly. Moments later, he frolics the same way with a favorite dolphin toy, a mangrove seed pod known locally as a horsetail. Rick cavorts like this for several days.

PICTURE 136

Driven to unusual heights by her courtship with Puck, Sylvia does an ex-
treme spyhop. In this picture, she appears to be performing the trained
behavior of the captive dolphin prancing backwards by pumping its tail
called tail-walking. She is not. I have never seen a free-ranging dolphin
tail-walking at sea.

Courting dolphins like Rick and Sylvia often use exaggerated behaviors around potential mates. Exaggeration draws attention from other dolphins as it alerts researchers to potential courtship activities. Relaxed exaggeration suggests good spirits. In contrast, agitated exaggeration suggests pain and fear, as in the next chapter.

CHAPTER 9

Writhing to be Free – The Torment of Entanglement

Exaggerated aerial behaviors do not automatically indicate good spirits. Ominously, exaggerated bowing, bracing, racing, breaching, spyhopping, and slapping may mean torment.

One late October day, the waters of the "Enchanted River" were a colorful carpet of red, orange, and brown leaves. We came upon a shy dolphin mother we call Valiant, named for

PICTURE 137
Tormented, 8-month-old Vidalia writhes to remove monofilament fishing line that had become wrapped around his body… to no avail.

her heroic survival of a shark bite, and her little boy Vidalia. They were showing the standard behavior in which the mother dolphin hunts and the calf, too young to hunt for itself, amuses itself nearby.

Unhappily, theirs was a cruel version of this standard seaside behavior. Little Vidalia swam nearby his mother but was not amusing himself. He was writhing, entangled in a painful cobweb of discarded fishing line. Wild with agitation, the little dolphin struggled with aerial behaviors to remove the body noose that sliced his skin and the maddening remoras that crawled all over him.

Vidalia struggled against the fishing line with every aerial behavior he knew, even leaping. He did partial headstands and intention tail slaps. He swiped the water with tail whips. He spyhopped into body slams like a falling tree. He did darting breaths like a reckless newborn, as if he reverted to infant behavior in the torment of entanglement. He did bent-head spyhops as if trying to wiggle out of the noose. He did countless side head slaps. Just as his mother Valiant had thrashed in the pain of her fresh shark bite, the little tormented dolphin rolled and writhed and smacked himself against the water.

Vidalia would struggle until he was exhausted and then swam "quietly" to catch his breath before renewing his futile fight with the unmoved fishing line. He strained against his entanglement pointlessly.

After Valiant finished hunting, mother and son meandered side by side. Seeking creature comfort, Vidalia kept trying to touch her. He leaned against her, rubbed along her, even tried repeatedly to clamber onto her back the way a baby monkey rides its mom like a jockey.

PICTURE 138
Vidalia's mother Valiant was a shy female, timid with other dolphins and with people. Yet, she trusted us to capture her son Vidalia and cut off the fishing line that entangled him.

It was painful to see him struggle. I wondered what his mother Valiant thought about all this. Capt. John wondered aloud, "Vidalia has to be crying at times, correct?" Superficially, the mother dolphin's behavior suggested that she had no idea of his struggles because she went about her business. But not entirely. For example, having her son clamber onto her back was uncommon in her life. Yet, some of the pictures of Vidalia clambering onto her back show her pausing and watching him with backwards glances. Another picture series of Vidalia riding on her back also shows how she sunk below the surface and rose again with him still in place; this required special effort on her part. She did what she could. But neither she, nor his wild writhing, could set him free.

Dolphin rescues are dangerous. They require dozens of marine mammal specialists and their boats along with the reasonable cooperation of the dolphin slated for rescue. One gray November morning as told in my book, Secrets behind the Dolphin Smile, we finally caught Vidalia, cut off the fishing line, and set him free. Vidalia's story has a happy ending.

Later that afternoon, Vidalia was again jumping around. This time, however, experienced dolphin observers Capt. Jack Steeves and First Mate Lani Grano felt sure that he was jumping for joy.

***

The mother dolphin's behavior after Vidalia's rescue was even more humbling: Valiant stopped what she was doing to come over and swim beside us briefly whenever she saw us for the rest of her life. It was her way of saying, "Thank you."

Vidalia did not play while he was entangled. That meant he did not surf either, the subject of the next chapter.

CHAPTER 10

Why Dolphins Surf Boats

PICTURE 139
*Dolphins are the only animals I know who come out of nature to play with people and to help people. Dolphins usually play with people by **surfing** the waves of our boats, formally called **assisted locomotion**. Dolphins probably surf boats mainly for fun, similar to people riding carnival rides for fun. Yet, dolphins may have other reasons for surfing too, some quite unexpected.*

Surfing: Yachts of Fun

How dolphins surf boats depends on the design of the boat. Dolphins can surf the waves off the back of boats and the front of boats. They can surf the voluptuous rounded rollers that glide perpendicularly off heavy yachts plowing through shallow sections of the "Enchanted River."

PICTURE 140
The delighted blond in her bikini on her yacht snaps photos of the dolphin Trix leaping from the yacht's wake. The horizon shows the open spans of the bridge whose construction launched this study.

PICTURE 141
*Dolphins can surf the wake waves off the back of boats, behavior called **wake riding**, as Sybil does on a crystal blue November day.*

PICTURE 142

Dolphins who wake ride behind the boat may surf at a safe distance from it. However, they sometimes surf cringingly close to the transom and outboard engine's whirring propeller, as Sylvia demonstrates here.

PICTURE 143

Dolphins can surf alongside a boat too. Here, Courtney surfs the port side of a broad-beamed craft that plowed the water into perfect mounds for surfing.

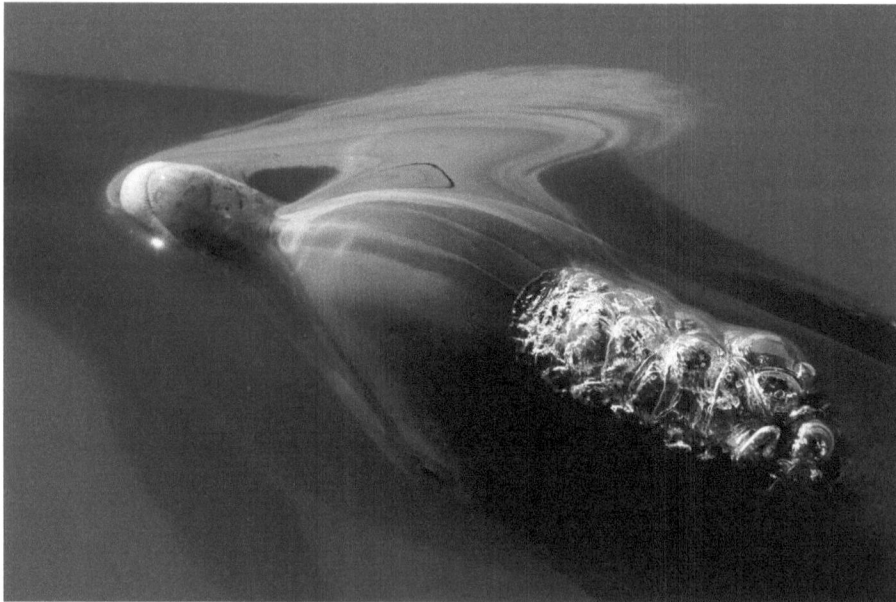

PICTURE 144

*Dolphins can surf the bow waves off the front of boats, behavior called **bow-riding**, giving awed observers who gape over the boat railing time to drink in the elegant delphinid form. As Cutlass' breath-defying close-up shows here, a dolphin bowriding through still waters is a magnificent natural image.*

A slow flow like Cutlass in Picture 144 takes more effort to balance. Slow surfing dolphins augment leisurely rides by pumping their peduncles more often and weaving, similar to skiing down a snow-covered ski run slowly. Some surfing opportunities are considerably slower than others.

Surfing: A Fable for a Fool

Cutlass' breath-defying close-up in Picture 144 is a stunning portrait of a bottlenose dolphin relaxing next to a boat she trusts. Trust like hers is expensive because it is only earned by a tremendous investment of time. Boats and boat-based observations of dolphins are expensive, too. Fortunately, many coastlines provide viable alternatives to boat-based dolphin studies: cliffs that offer sweeping aerial views of the spangled seas below and, if one is lucky, dolphins swimming through them. Different views have different advantages.

The tall breakers that topple and spatter white froth on the beaches off the cliffs overlooking La Jolla are popular with people and dolphins for surfing. Southern Californians and dolphins surf the same way: They line up in likely spots, race to catch a wave as it sweeps by, and slide down its face as it rolls to shore. They share waves too, often surfing side by side.

When it comes to surfing, people and dolphins mainly differ in how they end a ride: People ride the wave into shore and paddle back out past the breakers to catch the next wave. Dolphins never ride the wave into shore. Instead, they turn and leap out of the back of it before it crashes.

Watching dolphins during the spring and autumn months from the cliffs, we often saw gray whales migrating through, too. They seemed so solemn, plowing slowly past beyond the

PICTURE 145
View of surfing dolphins from the tall cliffs overlooking La Jolla in sunny San Diego, California. In addition to boat-based observations, I also studied dolphins from the cliffs as often as possible.

breakers and never trying to surf. I decided that the whales were too big to surf the breakers but that dolphins were the right size to surf the breakers and must have transferred that knowledge to surfing boats. After all, dolphins had been surfing for centuries before boats were invented. They must have learned from the breakers.

Then a college professor told me that dolphins surfed off the heads of gray whales. I snorted skeptically and wondered how big of a fool I appeared to be. Gray whales swim too slowly for a dolphin to surf. Any fool knows that.

I remained unconvinced about this fanciful dolphin-whale connection until the day on the cliffs when I saw a gray whale plowing past with bottlenose dolphins surfing the waves off either side of its bulky head. As so often happens in my life, the claims about which I am the most skeptical visit me in person, as if Gaia herself was conscious enough to whisper secrets when I need them. Just for emphasis, I saw the same behavior again in Baja in the gray whales' birthing lagoons.

Those gray whales might be slow, but they evidently shove enough water aside to create pressure waves that a dolphin is slick enough to surf. However, when it comes to surfing, in addition to how each ends a surfing ride, one suspects that surfing off the heads of whales is probably another difference between people and dolphins.

Surfing: Sharks

Bottlenose dolphins surf more than breakers, boats, and gray whales. I watched them surf off the waves created by the massive heads of whale sharks in Baja too, although the dolphins quickly lost interest. Perhaps this was because, searching the sun-drenched photic zone for microscopic meals to gulp down, the gentle filter-feeding giants meandered in all directions instead of plowing in a straight line.

PICTURE 146
This is the head of a young whale shark that is gulp-feeding at the surface in the rich waters of the Gulf of California, Baja. Its youth is indicated by the brightness of its dappling.

When I see dolphins bowriding off the front of our boat, I think of dolphins surfing off of the heads of gray whales and the occasional whale shark that is sufficiently roused to make speed. When I see dolphins wake riding off the back of our boat, I think of dolphins across the centuries surfing breaking waves.

***

PICTURE 147
Dolphins share the seas with other surfers, too. Black diving birds called crested cormorants (left picture) occasionally surf to hunt, seizing unsuspecting prey by sliding on a wave rushing up the beach. Manatees (right picture) surf too, occasionally sliding down a boat's wake waves.

***

Seizing Waves of Opportunity

Behaviors like surfing off the massive heads of whale sharks and gray whales show that bottle-nose dolphins are able opportunists who capitalize on local opportunities. People are able opportunists too, although we turn local opportunities into local customs. Might dolphins do the same?

Surfing: Cultural Differences

Surfing is natural for bottlenose dolphins because it matches their streamlining and opportunistic psychology, but like any behavior, it is honed by local ecology: tall handsome breakers that crash on the shores, short swells that roll in from pushy offshore winds, or exotic sea creatures and boats that are suitable for surfing.

These ecological conditions differ across different shores and, with them, the inclination of local residents to surf. For the same reasons I met countless human surfers in Southern California but none in west central Florida, it seems to me that different communities of bottlenose dolphins have different surfing cultures. Caveats to this proposition are the limits of my personal experience with surfing dolphins and the 'surfing suitability' of research boats I happened to occupy. For example, even the pluckiest calf in Carolina never tried to surf our sturdy, inflatable Zodiac.

San Diego bottlenose dolphins are avid surfers. Tall, handsome breakers crash up and down the Southern California coastline, providing regular opportunities to surf (Picture 145). Correspondingly, the dolphins are easily enticed to surf. They body-surf offshore too, launching with a unique "snap" of their powerful peduncles into smaller swells created by strutting offshore winds. Boats were rare in our study area at the time, yet the dolphins were easily

PICTURE 148
It was Florida dolphins' choosey surfing behavior that alerted me to the idea that they surf boat waves for fun, similar to the way people ride carnival rides for fun, but might also use boats as tools for other transportation needs.

persuaded to surf them too. Our sturdy Boston Whaler was suitable for surfing. To find dolphins, all we had to do was speed up. They appeared out of nowhere to surf our boat.

In contrast, west central Florida bottlenose dolphins are choosey surfers. Because the submerged offshore landscape of the continental shelf is angled too gradually to create big crashing waves, the local Gulf of Mexico coastline usually undulates with stubby swells that merely topple into unassertive breakers. Correspondingly, it is hard to entice local dolphins to surf boats. Our research boat Ms. Behavin' is a reasonable surfing boat, although we discourage the dolphins from playing with us, making their requests to surf us even more alluring. We do, however, have a number of splendid, surf-able yachts from which to choose.

Southern Baja bottlenose dolphins off the coasts of La Paz are occasional surfers. There, the coastal ecology has breakers as modest as west Florida. There were very few boats at the time I lived there. We studied Baja dolphins from a panga, an efficient broad-beamed "canoe" with a flat transom. Pangas are tough as nails but unsuitable for surfing. Only on rare occasions did determined Baja bottlenose ride our wakes.

The waves that hit the beaches of western Grand Bahama are generally too small to surf, yet an alternative is a nearby raceway called the Gulf Stream that could introduce local dolphins to the rush of speed. Grand Bahama dolphins are ready surfers, in part because our 80-ft (24 m) research yacht created irresistible waves at speed on a schedule that local dolphins had learned to anticipate.

Finally, near shore and intracoastal North Carolina dolphins are shy surfers, although the Atlantic seaboard is superb for body-surfing. Buzzed by countless boats, these dolphins were generally difficult to approach at the time I lived there. In addition, our solid-bottomed Zodiac research boat was unsuitable for surfing.

PICTURE 149
And, if this treasure trove is wanting, the view of a surfing dolphin is a guaranteed adrenaline rush! Yet, as this chapter hints, dolphins may sometimes surf for more than just fun.

In addition to differences in surfing cultures, it also seems to me that surfing reflects intelligence. For example, surfing is assisted locomotion. If a tool is defined as an object designed to serve one purpose then used to serve a different purpose, does that mean that dolphins use waves, whales, and boats as tools and surfing is some form of tool use? Waves neither break nor whales swim so that dolphins can surf them. Capt. John does not drive our boat so that dolphins can surf it. That is, surfing dolphins use waves, whales, and boats for a different purpose than that for which they were designed, like using a kitchen knife as a screwdriver or a safety pin as a fishing hook. Dolphins also transfer natural surfing to a variety of watercraft, showing flexibility and the ability to generalize.

Surfing: Swell Lessons Start Early

Surfing is a basic part of the dolphin skill set that starts early on the "Enchanted River." How early depends on mother. A few mothers are enthusiastic surfers, and their calves start surfing when only days old. Other mothers are sluggish surfers and may not take the calf surfing for months.

PICTURE 150
Jay is an enthusiastic surfer and takes her calves surfing their first weeks of life. Here, her experienced two-month-old calf Jacamo easily leaps out of the froth for a breath alongside mother. Jay also took Jacamo to see a manatee and let him play with baby sharks.

Surfing is a basic skill, but I did not appreciate how basic it is until little twisted Twig surfed alongside its mother Sabine (we never discovered Twig's gender). Twig was partially paralyzed from birth. The back portion of its peduncle was immobile and did not flex. The paralysis forced Twig to do a full or partial headstand every time it needed to dive, like a perpetually sounding whale. Sounding to dive was hard physical work and, pouring its resources into swimming, Twig stayed small and painfully thin.

PICTURE 151

Propelled by a boat's pressure waves, tiny Twig is able to surf alongside schoolmates despite its paralysis, though never able to leap into the air as surfing dolphins inevitably do. The view of this tiny disabled dolphin surfing that gray November day was a touching testimonial to the "assisted" part of "assisted locomotion."

Surfing: Finally Playing after a Long Illness

Human children do not play when they are sick or wounded. Similarly, baby dolphins do not play when they are sick or wounded. The baby dolphin Ballou was very sick. She was born in 2011, the year after the British Petroleum (BP) oil spill poisoned a massive portion of the Gulf of Mexico. Most of our dolphin calves born in 2011 died. The few survivors developed terrible skin conditions, like some horrible maritime measles. Bette's daughter Ballou was one of them.

Sick calves do not play. During the two years that Ballou was sick, she mainly swam at her mother's side. We saw her play only once, bouncing up and down in rare spyhopping water play. We never saw them surf either (of course, this is only during our observations). Although it seemed to me that Bette and Ballou never surfed because Ballou was sick, we had known Bette for eight years before Ballou was born and during that time Bette had been an occasional surfer at best.

Bette was an attentive and responsive mother. Ballou was strong. She finally healed when she was two years old. Her skin returned to the glistening pewter gray of healthy bottlenose dolphins, though she remained lighter in color than most. This was when we saw Ballou surf for the first time. Mother and daughter asked to surf by weaving under our bow like normal dolphins. After we sped up, they surfed and leapt out of the wake as if they had been surfing for years.

Unfortunately, sick baby dolphins miss out on more than play. They miss out on vital lessons of survival and seem to remain naïve to the dangers of life at sea. Within days of her recovery and triumphant surfing day, young Ballou vanished.

PICTURE 152

Ballou, shown in the foreground, had a serious skin condition for half of her life. On her sides, large white patches appeared as if the gray skin was scraped off. On what remained of the gray areas, white lesions erupted everywhere. As the months went on, her entire body color faded until she appeared to be bleached. In contrast, healthy bottlenose dolphins are a uniform, medium to dark gray color on the upper half of their bodies that fades to white on the undersides as a natural form of camouflage called countershading. In the background of this picture, Faye shows the color of a healthy dolphin.

PICTURE 153

Ballou recovers from a long illness and surfs for the first time when she is two years old. It was gratifying to see her finally playing like a healthy dolphin.

Surf: A Mourning Mom Surfs to Cope?

We found the dutiful mother Bette a week later, now alone. She wove under our bow in a mute request to surf. We accelerated.

Bette surfed the next time we saw her too, and the next. In fact, with few exceptions, we saw Bette surfing wildly for months. Bette switched from an occasional surfer to a compulsive surfer after Ballou died.

This unmistakable change in Bette's behavior was directly linked in time to her calf's death, but it was not Bette's only loss. Across the slow months of the calf's recovery, Bette and Ballou were in the near-constant company of another mother-calf pair, Faye and her calf Facet. Two weeks before Ballou died, Faye and Facet were killed by a boat that ran them over. It was in the wake of these three abrupt deaths that Bette became a compulsive surfer.

Her compulsion eventually faded. As of this writing six years later, Bette is once again an occasional surfer at best.

Readers can decide for themselves whether or not Bette was a mourning mother who surfed compulsively to cope with the abrupt deaths of all three of her closest companions.

***

Surfing for Fun: Boats as Carnival Rides

Most of the time, surfing dolphins are playing. Judging from these episodes, dolphins surf boats for the sensation, similar to the way people ride carnival rides for the sensation.

PICTURE 154
This is Bette surfing the first day we found her after Ballou died, leaping again and again and again with unusual vigor as shown here.

Surfing: Exhilaration

The animated dolphins who materialize to surf a boat's waves electrify the people on board, who then rush pell-mell for a place to watch the grinning surfers. Maybe the dolphin's riotous ride helps us relive our best roller coaster memory, screaming like a kid again. Most people are thrilled by surfing dolphins.

Individual dolphins vary tremendously in their keenness to surf. For example, Diana is a calm dolphin. She rarely fights. She rarely cavorts. She is fond of calves in general and conspicuously affectionate with her own. Three years into our study, we had yet to see her surf.

Early one morning in June, she hunted for breakfast off a favorite mangrove isle. The waters were calm but the dolphin was animated, unusually so. She peppered her hunt with headstands and wiggled with body shivers. We did not know that she was newly pregnant.

Later that morning, a handsome yacht powered up out of a no-wake zone two miles away. By the time it pulled abreast of Diana, it had worked up a good head of steam and a magnificent wake of voluptuous rollers into which the dolphin dove without hesitation.

"She's going to ride!" we cried. It was like a person springing from their desk onto a shrieking roller coaster.

Capt. John shot into action. Accelerating, he paced the charging yacht ahead of the rollers. Bracing, I aimed the camera eagerly. Diana slid down the roller like a slide, her silhouette shimmering intermittently through its translucence.

Faster and faster, Capt. John and the yacht captain cut a parallel course at speed. Diana shot free again and again, launching and landing. How could she recover fast enough to stay in that surging swell? She managed - and made it look easy.

PICTURE 155
Diana shoots free of the wake and twists, landing on her right side. Demure Diana was actually surfing!

A jet skier zoomed in, hit the wake, and went airborne like the dolphin. That man knew how to work those waves. Dolphin and jet skier played them, bouncing aloft, catching the next.

Yacht, yachters, researchers, jet skier, and dolphin sped on and on - everyone in sync, everyone riveted, everyone captivated. Diana surfed and leapt for over a mile. I think human hearts leapt every time she did.

As all exhilaration eventually ebbs, in due course the yacht slowed for the next no-wake zone. Electrified by the dolphin's wild ride, yachters, researchers, and jet skier bubbled with delight. Why is it so absurd to suggest that Diana was exhilarated too?

***

Sound ripples easily through water as undulating waves of pressure. Accordingly, sea creatures have excellent hearing. Dolphins hear an approaching boat for minutes before it arrives and may learn to recognize good surfing boats by mimicking other dolphins. When a boat approaches that the dolphins intend to surf, they usually wait where they are until the boat is abreast and then either station to catch it like human surfers or drop what they are doing and dash over to it at speed. I inevitably surge with anticipation when watching dolphins prepare to catch a ride on a passing boat.

Surfing: Urge to Surge

To me, surfing shows bottlenose dolphins' psychology of spontaneity. Yet, planning is sometimes involved, and perhaps some mysterious communiqués too, suggested by the dolphins' seamless coordination.

PICTURE 156
The perfectly-positioned dolphins catch the first roller and surge past inside an envelope of translucence. They ride their natural roller coaster into the shallows until waving sea grasses reach up and tickle their bellies.

It was mid-morning and gorgeous, before that part of Florida summers when the heat is pounding by 8 a.m. Five dolphins, scattered across a shallow cove wrapped around an isle of mangroves, hunted for breakfast. It is hard to take pictures of hunting dolphins because one cannot predict where they will surface next. So I idled nearby, watching for the occasional dark dolphin silhouetted against shimmering, light blue waters.

In the distance, a yacht gradually accelerated out of a no-wake zone. I heard its engine faintly. The dolphins heard it too, undoubtedly more clearly than I did. A few minutes later they stopped hunting, bunched together, and milled around a small area just off the watery path that the distant yacht would eventually take if it passed this way.

Gaining speed, the yacht steamed towards us. Yet like some Einsteinian thought puzzle, the closer it approached, the slower it seemed to go. In impressive coordination, all five dolphins lay together at a perpendicular angle to but facing away from the yacht's eventual course. They reminded me of human surfers in San Diego lining up to catch an incoming wave.

Finally, the yacht thundered by. The great round-topped waves of its wake rolled at us one by one.

They heard. They planned. They waited. They rode.

Then they resumed hunting. (They went back to work!)

Surfing: Waiting for Disney

When dolphins drop what they are doing to surf, it illustrates their opportunistic psychology. When they station and wait for an approaching boat, they have a plan for a few minutes into the future. However, they may make longer plans.

One tranquil autumn day, Queen Priscilla and her son Puck milled in the narrow waters between a jutting point of land and a small man-made junk spoil piled up from Army Corps of Engineers dredging in the 1960s. Drake joined them some minutes later. Lulling, the three dolphins rolled and nudged each other casually. Soon Xanadu and Sybil arrived with their calves and joined the others in casual nudging. The seven lulling dolphins swam without going anywhere or doing anything other than creating an appealing tableau of gray bodies in green waters against blue skies.

A yellow dot appeared on the distant green waters. It meant trouble for me. It was an over-sized boat, notorious for throwing the biggest wake of any local vessel, and its captain was a bully about it. His claim was that he had passengers to please and was simply in search of dolphins to entice to surf. Other boats best get out of his way. On the other hand, it meant a delightful surfing boat for the dolphins, and right on time, too.

The distant dot grew as the notorious yellow boat approached. It was time for me to leave the narrow strip of water where I watched the appealing tableau of lulling dolphins going nowhere, doing nothing. If I stayed where I was, the yellow boat's big wake would flip my little boat over.

The notorious yellow boat raced closer. I moved away. The dolphins stopped socializing and lined up side by side facing it, ready to rush it. When it came abreast, they disappeared into its mighty wake and rode it down the way.

PICTURE 157

Passengers onboard the notorious yellow boat scream happily at every sil-houette of a dolphin flying out of the froth like this. Whether leaping alone or in tandem, each dolphin dragged one fluke in the water the way a leap-ing dancer always knows the distance between her foot and the dance floor.

Dolphins of the "Enchanted River" do not have schedules that we know of, but the notori-ous yellow boat was scheduled like a city bus. The dolphins had been doing something during their appealing tableau of gray in green against blue: waiting for the notorious yellow boat, akin to people waiting at a bus stop.

Dolphins are masters of movement, in transit 99.9% of the time. That leaves few occa-sions that they meander in one spot – swimming without going anywhere, as they had this day. Their relative immobility is a clue that they might be waiting for someone or something. It is gratifying to be able to wait and see with them.

***

Our longest surfing episode on the "Enchanted River" involved a trio of dolphins who surfed for half an hour! After it ended, the dolphins swirled around our boat for several more minutes before continuing on their way. It was a prime opportunity to watch them for signs of heavy breathing after such exertion. There were none. Little wonder we call surfing 'assisted locomo-tion.' Surfing may be no more breathless than a taxi ride.

Surfing: Hailing a Taxi Cab

In my view, dolphins ask to surf. They usually ask our boat by weaving back and forth under its bow or swimming against its side. But there are other ways too. On occasion, they use the

PICTURE 158
*We were speeding south one early spring day when Fran suddenly leapt across our bow. We slowed. Fran leapt again as her son Fugazi came over. They stationed themselves behind the boat. Accommodating them, Capt. John accelerated steadily. Here, mother (in the water) and son (in the air) surf us all the way to the next no-wake zone. Fran **had** hailed us!*

seaside version of hailing a city cab from the curb with a waving arm: by leaping across the path of a speeding boat.

The eye-catching gesture of an individual leaping across one's path is not just a maritime invitation to play. My cat Chrissie invited me to play the same way: by flinging herself across my path as I walked through the house. In Chrissie's case, it was an invitation to play a chase game. Certainly, the dolphin leaping across the path of a speeding boat might simply be racing to jump into its waves without necessarily hailing it. But one wonders.

Surfing for Transport: Boats as Taxi Cabs

A basic difference between a breaking wave and a boat wave is where each goes. A breaking wave only goes to shore. A boat goes somewhere. Dolphins may understand that boats have destinations and provide faster transport than swimming, and take advantage of that.

This is suggested by the times that dolphins surf our boat until we come abreast of a bay with new dolphins in it, whereupon the surfers drop out of our wake and head over to the new dolphins as if that was the whole idea. It is possible that the surfing dolphins heard the distant dolphins and took advantage of our convenient presence to go see.

PICTURE 159

Dolphins may use boats as water taxis, a convenient way to arrive at a destination faster, as Diana does here. If so, dolphins hop a passing boat less like a modern taxi cab than like an old-fashioned streetcar.

Surfing to Safety: Boats as Get-away Cars

Dolphins may surf a boat to join other dolphins more quickly than they could by swimming, but they may also surf a boat to elude other dolphins more quickly than they could by swimming. One of the incidents that suggest that dolphins may surf away to safety involved two junior bulls dodging two senior bulls.

On a summer day with puffy clouds dotting blue skies like popcorn, a trio of dolphins was busy hunting. The trio included junior bull Scrapefin Sam, his bonded bull buddy Ski, and Sylvia, a young adult who recently blossomed into the maritime version of the attractive girl next door.

Abruptly, Scrapefin Sam sprinted a great distance away, too far to be chasing a fish. Two likely reasons for his abrupt exit soon surfaced: senior bulls Bruce and Drake. They oozed through the trio's hunting grounds with the privilege of higher dominant status. Evidently, upon hearing their approach, Sam had spooked and run.

Ski and Sylvia were following Sam when a passing yacht presented a timely alternative. All three shot into its frothy wake and surfed away. My question was whether they surfed away to safety.

The trio's hasty retreat when the senior bulls appeared was perhaps just a coincidence. Yet, given their histories, this episode read more like a soap opera. If it was not a coincidence, it suggested that the junior bulls understood that the passing yacht provided a speedy escape from the consequences of tangling with the senior bulls.

These four bulls had wrangled over dominance rank for years. At the time of this episode, Bruce and Drake out-ranked Sam and Ski. The latter also had toothrakes, which are signs of recent battle. Maybe Sam and Ski surfed away wisely to avoid another skirmish.

PICTURE 160

Maybe today's trio simply surfed away on the spontaneity of life at sea, and bottlenose dolphin social histories and relationships do not matter. It is more likely that histories and relationships do matter. Bottlenose dolphins are intelligent animals with complex relationships that last decades - plenty of time to forgive and forget, or to remember.

A skirmish was possible, because the relationship between Drake and Sam had seethed with conspicuous tension for years. For the first half of our 15-year study, Drake harassed Sam at every opportunity. On the few, more-recent occasions when they occur in the same social group, Sam remains wary in Drake's presence, indicated by darting around and remaining at a guarded distance.

Ski and Sylvia each had their own stories with the senior bulls, too. Years before, Ski and Drake were bonded bull buddies until Drake switched his allegiance to Bruce. Two years before today's incident, Bruce had courted Sylvia heavily until he summarily shifted his attention to another female, Faye, after she became abruptly available upon the grisly death of her calf.

Surfing: One Way to Say I'm Sorry

On the other hand, surfing together may be a gesture of unity. After Oliver's dramatic challenge to Nick and Rick (Picture 77), Oliver left our part of the "Enchanted River" for a year. Upon his return, he again engaged in a series of stylized skirmishes with Nick and Rick.

In a final contest, the three bulls wrestled in a congenial match that ended when they surfed off together on the waves of a passing yacht. Since then, the three bulls greet each other or join together without incident. I think his series of stylized skirmishes with Nick and Rick helped Oliver ascend several rungs of the bullpen social ladder. Oliver had made the grade.

PICTURE 161
Oliver, Nick, and Rick (not shown in this picture) surf together in a possible sign of unity.

Surfing: Swapping Surfers

PICTURE 162
One of the stranger facts about surfing is that surfing dolphins may swap spots. This occurs when one set of dolphins leaps into the wake of a passing boat, but a different set disembarks from it. This unusual feature is documented by pacing and taking photos of surfing dolphins to later identify the individuals who hurtled out of the froth. Who would suspect such a swap?

There are many unsuspected events at sea. A particularly memorable swap started when Bruce and Drake vanished into the wake of a passing yacht and ended when Jay and her calf disembarked from it. Recent winds had whirred soft sands off the sea floor and changed the color of the seas to mint mocha, milky enough to reflect the shadows of birds flying overhead, each a dark soaring cross.

We were photographing Jay for the record and searching for the missing bulls when the shadow of a colossal cross soared overhead. No passing pelican this! It was more like a 747 commercial airliner casting its shadow from directly overhead. Its wingspan stretched a hundred feet to either side of our boat. The body of the cross shaded us for several seconds. I clutched Capt. John's arm in alarm as we craned the skies in every direction for the source of the colossal shadow. Never saw an entity. Never heard a sound.

The only cloaking devices at the time were on the fictional TV show Star Trek and its offspring. Ever realistic, Capt. John made a brief reference to the nearby military base, "You're near MacDill, my dear. Your government dollars at work."

Surfing: Steer Clear!

No person can swim as fast as a dolphin can swim. But we can ski. A snow skier can bank and turn and carve down a mountain of sparkling snow framed by emerald fir trees and cobalt skies. A snow skier can flow. Dolphins flow for a lifestyle. One blessed ski run at a time, snow skiers share the dolphin's flow.

Just as snow skiers must watch out for each other to avoid collisions, dolphins who surf the same boat waves must watch out for each other too. Bette and Sylvia demonstrated this fine art during a ten-minute surf alongside a yacht. They leapt more than three dozen times during

PICTURE 163
Snow skiing is probably as close as a person can get to what it must be like to surf like a dolphin.

PICTURE 164
Bette and Sylvia surf nimbly without colliding.

that ride, alternating between individual leaps by one dolphin and synchronous leaps by both, the latter close enough in the air to nudge each other, but without mishap.

Dolphins are nicely designed to watch for other dolphins because their eyes are located low on the sides of the head behind the corners of the mouth (Picture 86). This placement allows them to see what is ahead, to either side, below, and some indication of what is coming up from behind them. Unfortunately, even this wide visual range may not be enough.

***

Surfing: Appalling Ocean Commotion

Snow skiing and carnival rides are fun but dangerous. So are boats. Boat captains can endanger dolphins in a parallel to the adage about fire arms: Guns do not kill people. People kill people.

Sometime during the excited action over the 4th of July weekend in 2015, the whirring blades of a boat propeller mangled the tailstock of a local dolphin we call Babyface.

The only positive element about Babyface's accident was that it was unprecedented. None of the marine mammal experts in our network knew how to respond to it because no one had experience with such a sickening injury. There were two options: Catch her and euthanize her or leave her alone to see what happens, perhaps giving her an antibiotic shot from a tranquilizer gun.

Why not rescue Babyface? The reasoning was that if we tried to capture, rehabilitate, and release her, the shock of capture could kill her. Another problem was that dolphins swim because they must. No one knew how to keep Babyface from pumping her tail until it healed. So the decision was to leave her at sea but keep an eye on her.

PICTURE 165

After the propeller of a passing boat brutally slices her tailstock open, Babyface compensates by doing headstand dives. Here, she raises her tailstock atypically; the added weight helps her submerge. Each gash from the propeller blade is deeper than the next. The cruelest slice is down to bone. It seemed impossible to survive. Her suffering was unfathomable.

Capt. John and I teamed up with federal, state, and local personnel and developed a plan to monitor Babyface without distressing her with daily encounters. To convalesce and recover at sea, she needed to be allowed to use her energy to heal rather than to be forced to waste it avoiding boats that were monitoring her welfare.

At first, the brutally wounded Babyface stayed in The Pass, the location of the bridge construction project that launched this study and where her mother Faye had raised her. During Babyface's childhood, we could almost guarantee seeing Faye and Babyface in that area. These familiar waters were probably comforting to her. As far as we know, she initially spent some time with big bulls Drake and Bruce (whose attention had sent her into aerial animation ten years before, see Picture 21) but otherwise stayed alone. This is standard for a wounded dolphin, similar to a sick cat hiding under the bed. I have heard alternative explanations for her solitude, however, such as other dolphins abandoning her because her obvious vulnerability attracted predators that increased their personal risk or simply because she could not keep up.

Miraculously, Babyface managed to catch enough food to eat. Dolphin metabolism revs like a race car. Dolphins who cannot stoke their voracious appetites starve in mere days. She lost weight but not gravely so.

A month after the injury, Capt. John and I were able to document that her behavior, unbelievably, was nearly normal and also how she compensated. Early compensation was to do headstand dives. Lacking standard peduncle power, she used the weight of her whole body to help her submerge. These dives morphed into dives in which she elevated her tailstock to

PICTURE 166
*Two years after her brutal accident, Babyface surfs up-side-down on a
passing swell. She is newly-pregnant with her first calf, which despite her
injuries she carried full term. Babyface survives as of this writing.*

atypical heights for the added weight. A second form of compensation was letting her peduncle flow out behind her, resting it whenever possible in behavior called a fluke flow.

Two months after her injury, Babyface had social companionship again. She spent one morning with sprinting champs Gazio and W.R. (Picture 78) until Nick and Rick chased them away. Social companionship was a good sign that Babyface was feeling better. Five months after the injury, Babyface had healed enough to tail slap would-be suitors (Picture 88).

Babyface is essential to the future of the dolphin community of the "Enchanted River" because she is a female. We need more females to counteract the statistically significant decline in females who left the area during bridge construction. No community thrives without mothers to produce young.

Babyface is also essential to future dolphins because she is a vital source of local knowledge. Babyface grew up along our stretch of the "Enchanted River." As a resident, she knows every nook and cranny. She knows how to survive here. She knows how to find food, when to go to the Gulf, and how to conserve energy in winter. She knows who to avoid, who to trust, and how to maintain her many social relationships – all knowledge that is as vital to a dolphin as how to find food. Dolphins must learn these and other survival skills; they are not inborn. They learn survival skills from more experienced dolphins, like Babyface.

***

PICTURE 167

Surfing is natural. Jumping is natural. Watching dolphins surf and jump is a delight. Maybe bottlenose dolphins really do live in the luminous present. Maybe our ancient human hearts, born about the same time as theirs some five million years ago, know it - but have forgotten how. Maybe, for that glowing moment when a dolphin jumps, we remember.

PICTURE 168

Until We Meet Again...

Solve the word puzzle on the next page.

1. Acoustics	35. Grass [Wearing]	69. Rest
2. Baleen	36. Growl	70. Right [Whale]
3. Behavior	37. Grunt	71. Rorquals
4. Beluga	38. Gull	72. Salt
5. Binoculars	39. Harbor	73. Scars
6. Blowhole	40. Harpoon	74. Science
7. Blubber	41. Humpback	75. Sea (3 times)
8. Boat	42. Hydrophone	76. Seabirds
9. Boney	43. Lake	77. Seal
10. Bottlenose	44. Lean	78. Sea Lion
11. Bow	45. Leap	79. Signature Whistle
12. Bowhead	46. Life With A Smile	80. Social
13. Breach	47. Lobed	81. Sonar
14. Bullfight	48. Marine Mammals	82. Species
15. Calf	49. Melon	83. Spectator
16. Camera	50. Minke	84. Stenella
17. Cetacea	51. Mullet	85. Stranding
18. Cetology	52. Mysticete	86. Tailslaps
19. Click	53. Notes	87. Teat
20. Countershading	54. Oceans	88. Teeth
21. Cousteau	55. Odontocete	89. Tern Thief
22. Danger	56. Orca	90. Toothrakes
23. Data	57. Pectoral	91. Tournaments
24. Diel	58. Peduncle	92. Toy
25. Do As I Do	59. Perch	93. Travel
26. Dolphin	60. Photography	94. Tuna
27. Dorsal Fin	61. Pinwheel	95. Vocalizations
28. Dorsum	62. Play	96. Water
29. Drum	63. Pod	97. Wave
30. Echolocation	64. Porpoise	98. Whale
31. Eel (2 times)	65. Propeller	99. Whaling
32. Feed	66. Recreational Sex	100. Xeno
33. Filter Feeder	67. Reef	101. Zoo (2 times)
34. Flukes	68. Research	

Word Puzzle of Marine Mammals and their Behavior

See if you can find 101 words about marine mammals and their behaviors listed forwards, backwards, up, down, diagonally, and even with some overlap! Like everything, try starting at the bottom and working your way up....

```
E X E N O B L U B B E R B J D E L I M S A H T I W E F I L O
L R A S E A B I R D S C E R U P I H T E E T E V A W X I D P
A E M B F K G D D L P A P A E L G R A S S U N T T Y Z O O E
H L N O L L R R O A O P T A G O R T N E A B D S E L N T P D
W L O W U H O H L R I T R N U N A S O N A R A U R T U E P U
C E O H K H W A P O S I E U O M T A I E C I N O O L B C R N
E P P E E Y L M H T R U A T B D I E L M S G G C R H O H E C
T O R A S D R V I C U I M D S K O J A G E H E A F A H O D L
O R A D N R B O N E Y T L N E L N R E H D T R E N R U L E E
L P H O T O G R A P H Y I U H S I F S I E U E M A B M O E A
O E T O H P T A I L S L A P S N G B O A F R D Z L O P C F G
G M N D A H R B O A T P E S E R R D Y H L Z P O R R B A R N
Y Y N G E O N O T E S Q D M A R S E K U L F W O W X A T E I
E S C I E N C E T A C E A Y I L G U L L L H I Y R V C I T D
N T C R W E D A T A S M V T A N U G A A O V E N U P K O L A
O I R A X O Q W L R M I U U H G K G C L A U T E A T O N I H
L C P E R U E L A A K V Q C N R U E E H L Y E D L O T I F S
E E L L A S O L L E S R A I A L A K E E O C L I C K E S S R
M T J R N S U S R P O E D S E L H B P E C T O R A L R C E E
A E I A I C U T E R R N S B L P J L A S O C I A L U N I J T
A U E T O Y R C X B A L E E N I R E S E A R C H I L T S H N
M C I N Z A I T E R A E N A A C O U S T I C S D D E H F G U
O E I M T E C E T C N E E M A M M G N I L A H W A B I R C O
S B Y S S T I S R M T I C O U S T E A U C A M E R A E R K C
S T L O B E D O T S A R O S B O T T L E N O S E H G F L I C
B F T T O O T H R A K E S Z E L T S I H W E R U T A N G I S
T E N T O U R N A M E N T S P I N W H E E L Z D O A S I D O
S E U B H R M Q V I V O C A L I Z A T I O N S I O P E R C H
E D R W R E C R E A T I O N A L S E X P X D R U M Y N N E P
R E G L E B U L L F I G H T Y S P E C T A T O R T E L L U M
```

139

Endnotes

[i] **Ann Weaver's Life List of Animals Experience**

PRIMATES: Allen's Swamp Monkeys, Bonnet Macaques, Bonobos, Capuchins, Celebes Crested Macaques, Cotton Top Tamarins, Douc Langurs, Drills, Goeldi's Monkeys, Gorillas, Hamlyn's Guenons, Kikuyu Colobus, L'Hoests Guenons, Mantled Howlers, Orang-utans, Pigtailed Macaques, Pygmy Marmosets, Red Howlers, Mandrills, Ring-tailed Lemurs, Squirrel Monkeys, Spider Monkeys, Talapoins, Woolly Monkeys

MARINE MAMMALS AND SEA CREATURES: Bottlenose Dolphins, Spotted Dolphins, Striped Dolphins, Common Dolphins, Pacific White-sided Dolphins, Elephant Seals, Sea Lions, Whale Sharks, Giant Manta Rays, Sperm Whales, Fin Whales, Blue Whales, Bryde's Whales, Pilot Whales, Risso's Dolphins, Manatees

CARNIVORES: Alaskan Brown Bears, Black-footed Cat, Canadian Wolf, Cape Hunting Dogs, Cheetahs, Chinese Wolves, Corsack Foxes, Cougars, Fennec Foxes, Fishing Cat, Grisons, Hyenas, Large-spotted Genet, Manchurian Brown Bears, Margay, Polar Bears, Red Pandas, Short-clawed Otters, Siberian Tigers, Sloth Bear, Small-spotted Genet, Spectacled Bears, Spot-necked Otters, Sumatran Tiger, Sun Bears, Zorillas

SMALL MAMMALS: Anteaters, Binturong, Dwarf Mongoose, Echidna, European Red Squirrels, Hedgehogs, Hutia, Hyrax, Kinkajous, Meerkats, Patagonian Cavies, Prevost's Squirrels, Tree Shrews

UNGULATES: Addra Gazelle, Altai Wapiti, Anoas, Axis Deer, Babirusa, Bactrian Wapiti, Baird's Tapirs, Barbados Sheep, Bawean or Kuhl's Deer, Bharals or Blue Sheep, Blackbuck, Chinese Water Deer, Cretan Goats, Cuvier's Gazelle, Dybowski's Sika, European Wild Boar, Formosan Sika Deer, Greater Kudu, Guanaco, Lesser Kudu, Manchurian Sika Deer, Mhorr Gazelle, Mouflon Sheep, Nilgiri Tahr, Nubian Ibex, Pampas Deer, Pot-bellied Pigs, Pronghorn Antelope, Pygmy Hippo, Red River Hogs, Roan Antelope, Roe Deer, Slender-horned Gazelles, Somali Wild Asses, Takins, White-bearded Gnu, White-lipped Deer, White-tailed Deer, Wood Bison

MARSUPIALS: Flying Squirrels, Goodfellows Tree Kangaroos, Koalas, Ring-tailed Possum, Tree Kangaroo, Virginia Opossum

BIRDS: Abyssinian Hornbills, Amazon Parrots, Barn Owl, Blue Jays, Brown Pelicans, Burrowing Owl, Caracara, Cockatiels, Cockatoos, Conures, Cormorants, Crows, Doves, Emus, Finches, Grackles, Great Blue Herons, Great Horned Owl, Guam Rails, Kestrel, Lesser Egrets, Lories, Lorikeets, Lovebirds, Macaws, Milky Storks, Mockingbirds, Moor Hens, Nighthawks, Night Herons, Ostrich, Pelicans, Pigeons, Pileated Woodpeckers, Quail, Red Knots, Red-shouldered Hawk, Red-tailed Hawk, Screech Owls, Spectacled Owl, Thrushes, Toucans, Trumpeter Swans, Warblers, Waterfowl, White Storks

REPTILES: Ball Pythons, Boa Constrictors, Dumeral's Boas, Corn Snakes, Cunningham's Skinks, Dwarf Chameleons, Florida Alligators, Garter Snakes, Gould's Monitor Lizards, Green Iguana, Hermit Crabs, Indigo Snakes, Jackson's Chameleons, King Snakes, Nile River Monitor Lizard, Rat Snakes, Rosy Boas, Taiwanese Beauty Snakes, Terrapins, Veiled Chameleons

FISH: Experience with freshwater and saltwater aquaria

DOMESTICS: Chinchillas, Domestic Goats (Saanens, Pygmies, Alpine, Toggenburgs, Nubians, LaManchas, etc.); Domestic Pigeons (Helmets, Tumblers, Chinese Owls, Etc.); Domestic Sheep (Shropshires, Karakuls, Colombians, Cheviots, Suffolks, Hampshires, Jacobs, Southdowns, etc.); Dexter Cows, Ferrets, French Lop Rabbits, Guinea Pigs, Llama, Horses, Malamutes, Miniature Horses, Mules, Neapolitan Mastiffs, St. Bernards, Tibetan Mastiffs

www.ingramcontent.com/pod-product-compliance
Lightning Source LLC
Chambersburg PA
CBHW041420290326
41932CB00042B/31